ALWAYS BEAUTIFUL

ALSO BY KAYLAN PICKFORD

Always a Woman

ALWAYS BEAUTIFUL

KAYLAN PICKFORD

PHOTOGRAPHS BY
J. FREDERICK SMITH
ILLUSTRATIONS BY
MICHAEL ARUNDEL

G.P. PUTNAM'S SONS   NEW YORK

G . P . P UTNAM'S S ONS
Publishers Since 1838
200 Madison Avenue
New York, NY 10016

Library of Congress Cataloging in Publication Data

Pickford, Kaylan.
Always beautiful.

1. Beauty, Personal.   2. Middle aged women—
Health and hygiene.   I. Title.
RA778.P58   1985   646.7'042   85-3707
ISBN 0-399-13018-7

Printed in the United States of America
2   3   4   5   6   7   8   9   10

Designed by Suzanne Noli

ACKNOWLEDGMENTS

I do not know the words to express the gratitude I feel to J. Frederick Smith once again for his contribution to this book, the second book he has so generously and graciously helped me with. His photographs have appeared in this country and abroad for the past twenty-five years and are known to be always beautiful.

I am awed by Carol Tonsing's wonderfully perceptive mind, which enabled her to so skillfully organize the mass of my writing for this book and to bring it into clear focus and order. I also thank her for the many suggestions and important additions I would otherwise have overlooked and left out. She is a superb professional and a delight to work with.

And many thanks to Michael Arundel for his fresh artistic talent and easy nature.

TO VICKY

Who cares, with love.

And to all the young women in my family who are in the process of
discovering that they *are* what they want to be, *beautiful*.

CONTENTS

ALWAYS BEAUTIFUL

RECOGNIZE YOUR BEAUTY

There is no one look for beauty.

There is no one time for beauty.

Beauty is now. It is always.

IT takes courage and effort to make changes in your thinking and your appearance. It takes real desire and it takes love, your own self-love. It also takes knowing how to make those changes. When those three things—desire, love and knowledge—come together as an inner force, you will project what you should have shown all along: that you are Always Beautiful.

While I know that beauty is the whole person, not just isolated parts, I wanted my physical self to shine, to be as glorious, as wonderful and as distinctively beautiful as possible. I wanted to be uniquely myself, to cultivate my own special look. I now know that my desire to improve my look is neither conceit nor vanity, but an obligation to the life force I have been given—to my own spirit, as well as those around me.

How I am, how I look affects others.

Doing what I can to improve myself, whether it is from the outside to the inside or vice versa, contributes to the whole of me. I consciously and deliberately *choose* to be as beautiful as possible. Every woman can choose exactly the same thing for herself. In this book I wish to share with all women what I have learned, and what I did in my quest to become as beautiful as I am able to be.

I believe that a woman's sense of her own physical beauty is as necessary to her as her breath, and that her perceptions of this beauty are deeply related to her understanding of herself and her life. I also believe that if you accept the all-pervasive negative judgments of others about the effects of aging, you will have a difficult time believing in your own beauty as you grow older and you may deny yourself the special joy of experiencing your very best self—at any age.

I am often discouraged or disheartened by a remark that is made all too frequently and always by a woman: "Well, it's all right for you to say what you do because you look the way you do, but for me and a lot of other women who aren't naturally beautiful it isn't so easy." The minute I hear a remark like that, I know something about the woman who made it, even though I may never have seen her before in my life. I know that she is probably discouraged with herself. Clearly, the whole *idea* of beauty is threatening to her. She is in trouble with her feelings about herself, and it is easier for her to disparage herself because of imagined "lacks" than to uncover the emotional injury *behind* that disparagement. (I always wonder if that same woman ever thinks about how easy it would be for the so-called beautiful woman to look like hell.)

But consider these facts. I was an obscure housewife who had never used cosmetics except lipstick until I was forty-three years old. I started modeling at forty-five and six years later was a top model. I used to say "top model in my age bracket," but now I just say "top model" when asked about my work.

There is no doubt in my mind that the few cosmetic changes and additions I made subtly improved my appearance and were a contributing factor to my becoming a model when I did. Maybe they were a major factor. I don't know. The small amount of self-help I learned to use *before* modeling did brighten my look and gave me a new glow of enthusiasm that encouraged me in every aspect of my life. *As my confidence grew, it gave others confidence in me.*

As a professional model, I learned a great deal more about the art of applied beauty. One of the things I learned was that it is *not* just the province of the young.

People did not seek me out as a beauty *until I started treating myself differently—positively—in my uniqueness,* until I made the decision to find and accept myself at my best, without comparing myself to the beauty of youth or the beauty of others. Comparisons can be deadly and damaging. Don't do that to yourself. While choosing to see the beauty in anyone or anything can't possibly diminish your life, it also includes discovering your own particular beauty. You are an original—miraculously unique.

Every woman can learn to enhance her special beauty if she is willing to give herself the time, the approval, the tools and the knowledge to work with.

At the time I started making changes, I was struggling with very fragile feelings about myself. I was shy and insecure, but I sensed it was more than just the lack of a robust attitude about myself. Those insecure feelings had been magnified, maybe even fostered, by a society that told me in no uncertain terms, through all the media for the past quarter century, that there is only one acceptable look of beauty—youth.

In my first book, *Always a Woman,* I described how a woman over thirty feels after she has been exposed to those twenty-five or thirty years of youth-oriented advertising. She is made to feel that she is not sexually viable or acceptable, and therefore is not beautiful or lovable. I gained firsthand knowledge of that truth when I started modeling at the age of forty-five. There were no photos or commercials that depicted a mid-life woman as beautiful or even active in a positive and wonderful way.

Businesses wouldn't advertise their products the way they do if it didn't work. And magazines, which, of course, depend on advertising to keep themselves afloat, are the adman's strongest allies. Nearly all women's magazines are aimed at the age group between eighteen and thirty-four, although some have recently extended their age barriers to thirty-six or thirty-eight, a few even to forty. But their visuals rarely deal with maturity. So life after age thirty or thirty-five is virtually ignored except for token articles about outstanding people who are miraculously going on, and even doing wonderful things with their lives. We learned to think these were the exceptions.

Because the mid-life woman was not advertised to or appealed to in any positive or beautiful way (and this includes fashion as well as beauty product photos), her feelings about herself were negatively affected both consciously and subconsciously. When I tried to find work as a model, I learned the established litany of advertisers. They couldn't use me or other models as they got older, they said, because older women do not want to see women their own age. They claimed that women who are, say, forty really think they are still twenty and don't want to be reminded they are forty and therefore not young (which, of course, might happen if they saw pictures of women in mid-life). And they claimed that if they advertised to the older market, the younger market wouldn't buy, but if they advertised to the younger market, the older market would still buy anyway. Captive audience. Captive market. Their billions of dollars' worth of research told them, so they said, that as people get older, they grow rigid in their buying habits. Which is to say that nothing new ever appeals to them.

But what was there to be flexible about? Nobody offered us anything to choose from. Nobody appealed to us.

Advertising had achieved a lot. All you had to do was say "middle-aged woman" and everyone in the country winced, including the women. Now we are finally beginning to see that we have allowed ourselves to be emotionally blackmailed by flawless, unlined flesh.

The years of youth "brainwashing" we were subjected to saturated our psyches much more deeply than most of us realize. For example, during interviews I am often asked, usually by a woman my own age, if I think I would be modeling had I not looked the way I do and stayed in shape. What kind of question is that? No one would ever pose that question to a young model. It is absurd, and it suggests that people are still amazed that any female past thirty-five can be considered beautiful.

And do you think women really let themselves go physically in mid-life more than men? I don't think so. That is just one more myth that has been perpetuated visually in print, on television and in films. Naturally men have not been anxious to disabuse us of this notion. We have seen many pictures of handsome older men, but almost none of beautiful mature women. This helps plant the idea that only a man grows handsome as he ages. That handsome older man is usually pictured with a beautiful young girl, an image that carries a double message, implying that there aren't any beautiful women his age and even if there were, young is better because young is beautiful.

Consider the power of these visual images. What if for the past quarter century, since the onset of television, we had seen only pictures of beautiful mid-life women instead of beautiful young girls? Almost everyone in the country would think mid-life was the best time for a female; young girls would look forward to getting there and would feel they had arrived when they did. They would be right.

So what have we learned?

We have learned to live in a state of pretend. We pretend every way we can that we are not growing older.

We have learned to be afraid of any physical changes that separate us from the idealized youthful images that saturate the media.

The mature woman still has to swallow the bias of the youth message at the very time in her life when she is wiser, richer, more mysterious and wonderful than ever. Those messages hit the young girl, too. She fears aging because she never sees the beauty and richness that can be her future self.

You cannot constantly think about what you are not and live your life in any rewarding way.

Beauty is the fiber of positive life.

Today, nearly everyone realizes that lack of physical conditioning plus mental boredom can breed psychological problems, nutritional problems, discouragement and even despair—emotions that are often associated with the idea of not being wanted or needed. But women in mid-life are becoming a major force in this country, and being out of condition mentally or physically robs us of our beauty at a time when self-love and self-nourishment could help us live wonderful, exciting new lives.

The country is undergoing a reversal in its demographics. The largest consumer market is now people in their late forties. By 1990, that market will be in its fifties, and by the turn of the century, one out of every four people in the United States will be sixty years of age or older. The buying power of the middle-aged market is already four times greater than that of the youth market.

Women's lives have changed because thay have sought change and because the demands and the economics of our society have changed. Women now comprise 54 percent of the work force in the country, a fact undreamed of when I was growing up. Women in mid-life, not on company payroll or financially independent, are searching for ways to express their creative energy and participate in life in areas beyond their homes. All of this has brought new awareness, new perceptions and the desire for new and better under-standing of ourselves. We are learning to fine-tune ourselves, and understand-ing how to bring out our beauty is the key to that fine-tuning.

I made the decision that I wanted to improve myself, but before I could make that decision, I had to acknowledge that improvement was possible. I had to learn to expand my thinking. I was evolving and I had to learn to keep up mentally, emotionally and physically. I did not want to hold on to a specific time in my life or a look that had passed. Beauty is fluid, ever in motion. Anything in nature will show you that, and we are part of nature.

Our beauty and our lives become one and the same. A complementary infusion of one into the other. Our thinking about mature beauty will relax and broaden as we learn to accept the truth of beauty in mid-life. Unlike youth, which is fleeting, our "look" and our *beauty* can be kept for years, even decades, once we have found our style and know how to keep pace with our physical changes.

The face of the nation is changing and will continue to change radically,

21

even dramatically. Mid-life, instead of being the age to dismiss or deny, is going to be the age to be. The face, not *of* the nation, but *in* the nation is going to be a mid-life face, and it will be a beautiful face. Yours.

Every woman today, particularly every woman in mid-life, should remember:

There is no one look for beauty.

There is no one time for beauty.

Beauty is now. It is always.

CLAIM YOUR BEAUTY

Beauty doesn't hold still
---
but changes with the seasons.

You have it no matter what season you're in.

I wanted to break out of my mold. Every woman does. It's part of the search. The search for beauty.

Beauty has been a subject for thought and discussion from the first moment a man or a woman felt that subtle emotion that stirs within us when we confront beauty in any form. Human beings have bought, sold, hoarded, demanded, stolen and searched for beauty throughout time. It is obviously essential to our minds, our hearts, our spirit. We can't and don't want to live without it. We want to see it, to own it, finally to be it. Why then are we so reluctant to see ourselves as beautiful? We look at ourselves and come to all sorts of negative conclusions. We know that whatever we are, we certainly are not beautiful.

When I was young, seeing another woman whom I thought was beautiful instantly made me feel self-conscious, awkward and shy about myself. Her very presence touched off the response that a female has to be beautiful to be. While those feelings remained undefined and unexamined, they became familiar over the years. I finally understood what they spelled out: inadequacy. Not enough. And I thought, If only, if only I were beautiful.

Today, as we grow older and grow further away from our youthful selves, we begin almost unconsciously to feel we have somehow failed. We have not remained physically young, in spite of all the advertising promises to the contrary. And we've been led to believe that if we don't stay young, we can't be beautiful. And if we are not beautiful, we simply do not exist or are invisible. But we do exist. We count. We are here and we are beautiful. And we have always been beautiful. After all, each one of us is the greatest miracle ever created.

One of the wonderful qualities of a woman in mid-life who is able to love is compassion, an all-important aspect of her beauty. Compassion is acquired through living and deserves a valuable place in the scheme of things. It should not be ignored. You should remember to use it toward yourself.

Maybe it's time for some changes.

If you haven't decided whether you are worth spending time on, doing what encourages your spirit and strengthens your beauty, you better decide, or time will take *you*. Youth has a look that says youth. Mid-life has a look that says mid-life. Until we are willing to reject the commercially acceptable definition of beauty, we will go on undermining ourselves needlessly.

We are conditioned to be defensive about our mature looks. In this day of instant communications, we often just sit back and accept new trends, the instant fashions or throwaway fads, that offer us nothing. We allow ourselves to be left out. We want instant cure-alls for everything, particularly our beauty problems. So we passively accept what is offered, and when we don't get results from so-called miracle products, we become disappointed and go back to thinking of ourselves negatively.

When we believe in ourselves, others notice. But first *we* must claim ourselves before anyone else will. This is particularly true if you are female, over thirty-five, and live in this country.

Everything in life has its opposite. If your thinking about yourself has been undermined, you can *learn* to think positively about yourself. It is important to find at least *some* balance between extremes, to achieve a firm and peaceful realization of self, which is essential to enhancing your beauty.

Beauty—it's putting all of

yourself in harmony.

I do all the things other women do. I have joined health clubs and quit, tried other things and quit those, too. Since I started using cosmetics, I think I have tried almost every product known. I watch what I eat, splurge, then feel guilty and pay attention again. I care. I want to look and feel my best, and when I do, I know I radiate beauty, if only because I feel beautiful, and that is an enchanted feeling.

That's what it's all about, isn't it? Sending out beautiful vibes.

As a model at my age, I am often under a fair amount of pressure, emotionally and psychologically. I know that if I don't come across in the camera, if I don't radiate, project energy and beauty for the creation of the photograph, the advertisers, the photographers, the art directors, the clients and the fashion people will be ready and quick to think: Ah, we knew we couldn't work with *that* age.

There is no one age, or one look, or one anything that can claim it alone is beauty. There are some "looks" that are better for commercial purposes than others. You can see by the ever-changing models that those looks are flexible as tastes and attitudes change. But in beauty, some ingredients are constant: energy, love and caring. This is the stuff of beauty.

To work as a model, I had to be able to be beautiful. That is, I decided I was able to express beauty. As much as anything else, beauty is a vibration, an electrical aura we project. We all have an aura and it is important that it be a beautiful one. Our own beauty is always available to us. As I have said, it is as close to you as your own breath.

If beauty is the sum total of your mind, body and spirit, put them in harmony.

Accepting your own beauty

---

is simply you accepting you.

Do it.

There is a voice out there saying, "I'm not beautiful. I never will be. I look in the mirror. I know." How many women treat themselves this way? Too many.

It is possible that when a woman like this looks in the mirror, she makes comparisons with an idealized image of how she thinks she should look, or of someone she'd rather look like. She can't win as long as she keeps that attitude.

Anyone who insists on disliking herself is only opposing herself. I am talking about a deep and chronic refusal to give *approval* to and accept yourself. You must be able to "see" yourself with love, for without that ability, you cannot demand beauty for yourself or your life. Secretly, in our hearts, I think we do demand beauty as a sort of God-given gift and we feel we have a right to it. But if we are at war with ourselves, if we appraise ourselves negatively, our understanding of how we can incorporate beauty into our lives will be limited. So will our ability to enjoy life. Beauty and joy go together. Disapproval and dislike do not go with joy—or beauty.

By the time you are in your middle years, you have learned a great many things about yourself that you did not know in your youth. That growth, what you have learned, has helped you define yourself. But if you become too set in your thinking, you may limit or undermine yourself. It becomes easy to reject new ideas or thoughts or looks for yourself out of hand. If you stop growing, you stay frozen in time.

Because change is constant, ongoing evolution, you have to observe it and how it relates to you, and not hang on to a particular hair style, or overly dramatic makeup, or no makeup at all, or aging fashion styles, or indifferent skin care or anything just because it may have worked for you at one time in your life. You hold yourself back at your peril. Allow yourself to continue discovering and using your full potential as you evolve with time.

Change does not always have to be dramatic, and in most cases probably is not. Often just simple additions or subtractions can make a real, positive difference. These can be small, subtle changes in your way of dressing, your hair style, how you put on makeup or even something as simple as your choice of colors.

I learned to question myself and listen to my answers and even to take some direction from myself. But before I began to make the visible, cosmetic changes, I made *invisible* changes because my natural pattern is to move from my inner self to my outer self. Your pattern and approach to yourself may be different. Everyone's is highly individual.

One important way to help yourself is to find and identify what you like or, better, *love* to do in life. Learn the ways you can use your special energy creatively. Know what is comfortable, encouraging and nourishing to you. I cannot think of anything that is more enriching and supportive to your spirit, your beauty, than that alone.

Not every woman is inclined to deep introspection, but almost every woman is willing to make some evaluation of herself if she believes doing so can make her more beautiful. I know I did. I looked at every aspect of my life, even the sleeping ones: my undeveloped, unawakened facets. I knew they were there, but I did not acknowledge them until my life altered and I was on my own. A mid-life woman alone.

I wanted then, and still want today, a wonderful, full and interesting life.

I wanted this to really happen, not to be just a fantasy. I wanted to be whole and beautiful, and since I knew that beauty was mental, physical and spiritual, I understood that all had to develop together.

What you do, how you perceive yourself, how you treat yourself, how you *use* yourself in society and how you allow society to use you—all affect you and therefore your beauty. It is vital that you learn to recognize which situations, conditions and people steal your energy, deplete or subtly drain you rather than add to your life.

I learned not to spend too much time with people who discouraged me because they had lost their vigor for life. It is too easy to think as they do because it is really the line of least resistance, and it can lead to negative habits and promote a lazy form of self-indulgence. There are literally hundreds of reasons that you may choose a way of life that is defeating (and you do choose, whether you think so or not). We all use the same excuses: too tired, too sad, too depressed, too lonely, no time, don't feel like it, who cares anyway, I'll do it tomorrow, I don't care. These are just a few of the regulars. Hear them! Where is the thought that says, even whispers to you that you do care?

I know it is easier not to confront yourself with questions. If you question, you might get answers, and there is a responsibility inherent in knowing the truth—you have to act on what you know. If you do, you are taking a big step forward for yourself. One thing is certain: Your life will not stand still. *To have any control, you have to act for yourself.*

If you were standing in a dark room you would look for the light so you could turn it on and see. Do as much for your inner life. Living requires energy and passion. So does beauty. Your appearance reflects your thinking and the state of your life.

You wear your attitudes.

Caring about your beauty

---

is caring about your life.

Let yourself know how much.

Others will know.

You are realistic. You know that nature will have her way, as she has since the day you were born. You know physical changes will continue as they always have as long as you are alive. You also know there are things you can do to help yourself stay in shape, not a nineteen-year-old's shape but shape for your time of life. You can keep pace as much as possible with your changes.

Emotionally and psychologically, you can focus on what is right with you, instead of what someone suggests might be wrong with you. You can think about what you have gained, how you have grown, what you have learned and how your looks have improved with age, lines and gray hair included.

I think women in mid-life are tired of being ignored on the one hand and insulted on the other by a society that insists on selling us one limited concept of what is beautiful and sexual and then claims this is what we asked for. Who asked? I think you didn't speak out for yourselves. But when you recognize and accept your own special beauty, the rest will come in the wake of your new understanding and your new confidence.

As advertising's youth cover breaks up and clears away (and it is disintegrating and drifting out at long last), as the atmosphere changes, a woman's mid-life beauty can become the brightest look on the horizon. It is a look that has been *over*looked, even though it is the most beautiful and sensual time of a woman's life.

The change will come when you know and acknowledge that you are what you are—Always Beautiful.

YOUR BEAUTIFUL FACE

> Beauty?
>
> You *finding* you.

I wanted my face to catch up with me.

I was in my early forties, living alone, when I decided on the basis of an instinct (someone else might say a whim) to move to New York City. I had no idea what I was going to do after I got there, but I knew I would change more than just my address. I had experienced years of emotional demands from others and I had adjusted and stretched, but now I was changing in response to *my* needs. Suddenly I had time to look beyond the immediate boundaries of home, and I had to wonder what the rest of my life was going to be like. I also wondered what I was all about, where I would fit in and—how did I look? I mean really look.

I started to observe myself apprehensively. Sort of peeking timidly. Searching.

I saw.

God, I had done that thing no woman is supposed to do. I had gotten older. I don't mean I thought I was a kid. I just had not paid attention to the physical changes that were taking place very naturally. Other considerations and emotional concerns had been so consuming that I had not had time for myself.

But there they were—changes. I could see new lines; the crow's-feet around my eyes had definitely deepened. The freckles were still there, which was sort of comforting, but my skin looked, well, just duller somehow. Not vibrant. The freckle-faced, rosy-cheeked kid had disappeared. But it was my eyes that hurt my feelings. They looked faded.

I knew that what I saw when I looked at myself was the truth. Truth in the sense that what I saw were facts. Older-face facts, if you will. I had given myself permission to really check out my look, but I wasn't just looking *at* myself, I was looking *for* myself.

I think that was one of the reasons I picked up and moved to New York City. I was looking for someplace to plug in, and although I didn't know exactly what I was going to do, at least I was doing something. I was forcing my hand. I was pushing myself toward life again. I wanted to be in life, alive in life. And I wanted to look alive.

If I could make changes in where I lived and how I lived, in my whole lifestyle, I could make changes in how I looked. It was time. Time for my outside self to catch up with my inside self. I had grown up a lot and was richer and smarter. I had learned a measure of compassion and thought I would use some on myself. I decided to start.

I look back now and laugh at my timidness. Childlike. But then, I felt like a child who was doing something she wasn't quite supposed to be doing— spending time on myself.

I was forty-three years old when I moved to New York City in 1973. The only beauty aids I had ever had were a jar of Vaseline, cold cream, some skin lotion, a comb and brush, an emery board and a few lipsticks. My idea of using cosmetics was using lipstick. How would I make changes on this outside me? Where would I begin? I began with what bothered me the most: my eyes. I wanted my bright look back again.

I noticed that small pouches had developed under my eyes. An inheritance. I knew they would only grow worse as I grew older, and they made me look chronically tired. I had the pouches surgically removed, and while I was at it, I had my top lids "trimmed" also. This immediately gave me a far more open, rested and relaxed appearance.

Next, I bought my first mascara brush and began to play. And play it was for a little while. I smudged under my eyes, sometimes above, and sometimes I managed to get it in my eyes. I didn't care. If others could learn to use mascara skillfully, so could I. I kept playing. I tried different ones. I got it on any way I could. No rules.

I was surprised by the change it created. I thought it was dramatic, and I loved it. I had never thought about my eyelashes, but now I realized they had faded after forty-odd years of exposure to the sun and elements. With mascara, I discovered small lashes guarding the corners of my eyes that I had never known were there. The faded tips of the larger lashes, when darkened, were longer than I realized. I learned how to frame my eyes, and, compared to their naked state, my eyes glowed.

It was both a fun and a serious change. Fun because it excited and pleased me, serious because it was an important improvement in my look that worked for me and will work for any woman.

For quite a while I felt as if I was just eyes. And then I investigated blushes. I hesitated about using color on my cheeks because I could remember in childhood seeing older ladies with bright red blotches on their cheeks that made them look like visitors from another planet. But today all those beautiful people used beautiful color—why not me? Why not?

The first color I tried was a very soft clear rose cream blusher (I have a slightly ruddy or pink-cheeked complexion). I was scared of overdoing it and put on such a slight touch of color that it kept disappearing. I was mystified until I understood it was being absorbed by my skin.

I grew bolder and then worried that all of New York was going to know I used cosmetics. Silly, wasn't it? How could I be so egotistical as to think anyone would notice, or give a damn if they did notice? I worried that someone out there whom I didn't even know would think I looked ridiculous. It's amazing how insecurity can make us think nonsense!

The truth is, I undoubtedly wanted to be noticed. Don't we all? But we want to be positively noticed. Maybe I still held that old-fashioned notion from my New England childhood that rouged cheeks and mascara would make me look like a hussy.

I tried different types of blushers and different colors. My face took on new life. I now had a fresh, healthy, just-in-from-the-cold look. Hussy or not, I loved it.

My eyes were glowing, my cheeks were pink again and I now wanted a mouth with soft lips. But those vertical lines that come with age and invade the edges of the top lip are intrusive and make it difficult to use lipstick. I found them unwelcome. I learned to use the new lip creams (lip fixes), which, when applied to the edges of the lips, help keep lipstick from running into those lines.

Then I learned to use a lip pencil to draw a soft outline along the edges of my lips. Widening those areas just a fraction, top and bottom, softens the appearance of any mouth, making it look a little bit fuller. The rest is child's play. With a lipstick, one that worked well with my natural coloring and chosen blusher, I filled in the lines I had drawn with the lip pencil, and soon I had a softer-looking mouth.

My brightened and improved appearance encouraged me and gave me a rising sense of confidence that hours of therapy might not have produced. And no one in all of New York City stopped and asked if someone had mistakenly let me loose in a child's paint box!

But I did begin to hear things like "What did you do, take a vacation?" and "I don't know what you are doing lately, but you look terrific" and "Beautiful." I began to hear that word, "beautiful," in connection with my appearance.

Then I knew. I was using that little amount of makeup in the right way. No one was ever sure what the change in my appearance was, but they saw a change. There *was* one—a good one.

I realized I had a delicious advantage in not having used cosmetics before in my life: I started at a time when they were really beneficial to me, really made a difference. A subtle but magic difference.

What you accept in thought,

---

you can become.

Become what you are—beautiful.

Discovering What Makeup Can Do for You: A Three-Step Basic Makeup That Works at Any Age

Those three basic steps—mascara, blusher and lip makeup—may be all you need to bring new life and glow to your face. This is minimal makeup—it's all I normally wear during the day—but it must be used subtly and skillfully. It must look as though it was a gift of nature. This may take a bit of practice, but you'll find it's worth the effort.

STEP ONE: WAKING UP YOUR EYES WITH MASCARA

What kind of mascara to buy: Look for the easiest, most basic mascara in a slender wand. You don't need the lash-building kind right now, and the old-fashioned mascara in cakes or tubes that comes with its own brush is very messy and awkward to handle. You want a mascara that slides on easily, has a rather thin consistency so it won't build up heavily on the lashes, and has

a slim brushlike applicator that is easy to maneuver. Also, keep a good supply of Q-Tips on hand. (You're bound to make a few mistakes at first.)

Colors: Stick to black or dark brown. Everyone can use black, but if you are extremely fair, you may want to try a softer shade like brown. Mascara now comes in many fantasy colors like violet and royal blue. Save these for special effects, if ever!

Before you apply: If you wear contact lenses, put them in your eyes. If you wear glasses, use a magnifying mirror to see what you're doing. And find the best, strongest light possible.

An easy way to put on mascara: Look straight into a mirror, with your chin lifted slightly. You can rest your little finger on your cheek for support. If your hands are shaky, you may want to experiment with mascara at a table so you can also support your elbow. I brush horizontally through my upper lashes first and then cover them from lid to tips, trying to touch every lash, even the little ones near the corner. Wait one or two minutes for this coat to dry.

Then lower your chin so you're looking up into the mirror. (If you were too hasty and your upper lashes have left a row of dots on your brow bone, remove the dots immediately with a Q-Tip.) Again looking straight into the mirror, apply mascara to your lower lashes, wiggling the brush back and forth to cover all the tiny hairs. Sometimes it's easier to work with just the tip of the applicator on the lower lashes, or to hold it vertically, sweeping back and forth.

Remember, the idea is to give all your lashes an even coat to bring out their natural length. You want to create a beautiful fringe, with every eyelash separate. If the lashes clump together, either you are using too much mascara or you may have selected a brand that is too heavy for your lashes. At most drugstores you can find a special tool with a tiny comb on one side and a brush on the other that can be very useful in separating lashes that stick together with too much mascara. An old toothbrush, a mustache comb or any fine-tooth comb will also work.

It takes a few minutes to put on mascara correctly, even if you're an expert, so don't rush. Get used to the feeling of the wand and how many coats your lashes need (I use two coats). When the buildup of the mascara looks phony, you have applied too much.

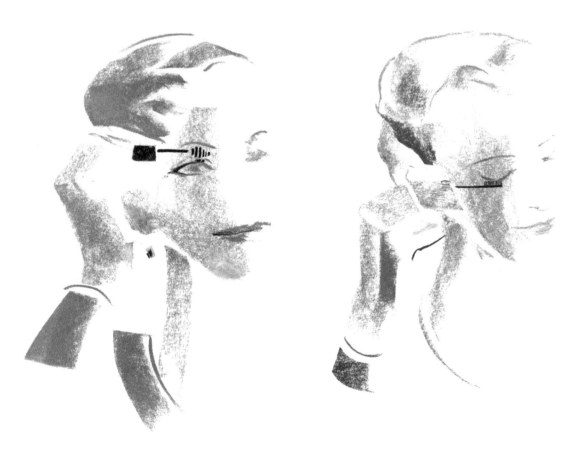

If your eyes become irritated from mascara, try another brand and check the ingredients. There are many hypoallergenic products available today (try a health food store). And to protect yourself from possible eye infections, don't use anyone else's mascara.

The life span of a mascara is usually three to four months. When it does not go on smoothly or flakes off your eyelashes, throw it away.

There are special mascara removers on the market, but you may not need one. Most mascaras come off easily with very gentle soap and water or with oil of any kind (baby oil, olive oil or cold cream). If you want to remove just your mascara, without disturbing the rest of your face, try dipping a Q-Tip in cold cream or oil and swabbing your lashes gently.

Some mascaras have conditioning ingredients built into them. To be sure your eyelashes stay soft and supple, a little Vaseline or castor oil on the tips at night will keep them in excellent shape.

Eyelashes, like any other hair on your body, may have become thinner by mid-life. It would be unusual if they kept the same thickness and density they had in your youth. But creating thicker lashes with mascara helps restore that look.

STEP TWO: FRESH HEALTHY COLOR FOR YOUR CHEEKS

What kind of cheek color to buy: The idea is to get the freshest, most natural, healthy-looking color on your face. For starters, try a powder blush in the lightest shade possible. You want a gentle color effect that will add sparkle to your eyes. You don't ever want color that calls attention to itself.

For applying and blending your blusher I recommend that you invest in a good sable brush. The best ones have a long handle (about five inches long) and silky bristles that feel good to the touch (about one and a half inches long) and cost about five dollars. The brushes that come with the blusher often aren't good enough. They're much too small for the diffuse, soft coverage you want, and they may feel very harsh on the skin. With a good brush, the blushing powder slides off the sable hairs, so you won't have too much buildup of color. You can find terrific sable brushes in an art supply store if your local drugstore or department store doesn't carry them.

A word about cream, gel or liquid cheek color: These are easy to blend with the fingertips and you can get a soft misty look rather than a "dry" look, but they are often difficult to control. It's very easy to get too much color on the face or a line of demarcation, which you want to avoid at all costs. The color also may have to be reapplied more frequently because it tends to disappear into the skin. But if you live in a climate with hot, humid weather, these may work best for you.

Colors: When you are just starting to use blush, get a very pale shade in a clean, clear pink, peach or rose. After you develop some expertise, you might want to try a darker coral, amber or burgundy for shading. Darker and very dark complexions can take deeper colors: reds with brown tones, browns and plums.

Where to apply color: Find your cheekbone and follow it with your fingertips to the point just under the center of your eye. Here is where you start to apply blush. Color should be darkest at this point and grow softer as you blend it back along the cheekbone and just under it to meet your hairline. No hard edges should be visible.

On a very narrow face, start a little more toward the side. On a very square face, place darker color just below the center of the cheekbone and slant your blush upward (to avoid a horizontal line of blusher).

STEP THREE: SOFT, EXPRESSIVE LIPS

Lip makeup has become very sophisticated, and it can do so much for your lips that it's worth getting a bit more complicated here. Using just a little dab of lipstick is certainly not the way to create a really wonderful mouth.

First, you'll want to *define* your mouth with a lip pencil. As we get older, the shape of our mouths can change. The corners tend to droop and the Cupid's bow curve may no longer exist. Lip liner pencil, less creamy than lipstick, gives you finer control over the shape of your mouth. Get one in a color that is a shade deeper than your natural lip color, like a pale burgundy-pink, or one that is two shades deeper than your lipstick. But remember, no harsh lines should show. You do not want a "hard"-looking mouth.

Color: Lipstick is usually best if it's clear and bright. Use a color that will help balance your eyes but not overpower them. For medium and fair complexions, try soft peaches, corals, pinks and roses. Darker and very dark skins can go for the more intense reds and brown or plum tones.

Before you apply your lip color: Consider using one of the lip fixatives, particularly if the weather is hot and humid, to keep color from bleeding and to help fill in those tiny lines over the mouth. These products really work.

To make a soft beautiful mouth: First, outline your lips with your lip liner pencil. Widen the corners a fraction to soften any droop. Then brush on lipstick color with a lip brush (or use it gently straight from the tube, blending it in with the liner so there is no demarcation line). Instead of lipstick, you may want to try a colored lip gloss. Used alone, the gloss can give a very soft, natural-looking color to the mouth. You can also use the lip pencil color all over your mouth, then top it off with a transparent gloss for shine. This way, the color will stay on longer, a good idea in warm weather or situations where you won't have much time for touch-ups.

Get a good lip pencil sharpener so that the point is always fresh and sharp.

To help out the shape of your lips: If your lips are narrow or very thin, line just outside your natural lip line and use a light color and gloss to make them look larger. If your lips are too full, line just inside your natural lip line and go easy on the gloss. Wear a very subtle color that blends with your complexion, so your mouth will not overpower your face.

Modeling: The New Old Kid on the Block

I thought I'd learned everything I was ever going to need to know about makeup for myself, but a year or so later, my life took a quiet but very dramatic turn. I began to model occasionally. No one asked if I knew how to model—thank God! I had never modeled anything. I knew absolutely nothing about it.

Talk about insecurity. I was the old new kid on the block, or maybe I was the new old kid. I didn't know what I was doing in front of a camera, but what added the greatest terror to my life was watching the lithesome young models show up at a job with full confidence, blithely sit down in front of the huge studio makeup mirrors with glowing lights, casually open their mysterious model bags and slowly begin to unload sponges, powders, eyelash curlers, eyeliners, eye shadows, Q-Tips, boxes of color for cheeks, lips and eyes, polish for nails, removers, emery boards, curlers, pins, mascaras, eyebrow pencils, highlighters, contour powders, cover sticks, bases, moisturizers, Kleenex, etc., etc., etc.

And I thought I knew something!

My three-step fix for my eyes, cheeks and lips was wonderful for my everyday life, but I saw very quickly that it was hardly suitable for professional modeling. I was going to have to learn it all if I wanted to work in the big time. I was going to have to learn it on the spot, in public, so to speak.

During the first years of my new career I was always relieved when I worked with other models because I could watch them do their makeup. I tried not to be obvious. The jobs I was really grateful for were the ones where there was a makeup artist present. I tried to learn exactly what he or she did, what was used, how it was applied, etc. Sometimes I didn't like the results, other times I did. I recognized that what I didn't like was a hard look. The hardness that comes from using too much makeup aged me in a way I didn't like. In fact, I liked my totally bare face much better.

Every makeup artist has his or her own technique and style for "doing" a face. When I started modeling in 1975, many of the artists were very young, and some had never worked on a face over thirty. I knew that when I was made up exactly the same way as a girl of seventeen or eighteen, I was in trouble. My older look, thinner skin and lines couldn't handle the intensity and opaqueness of too much makeup. It would take over my face and bury all the natural light in my skin, intensify lines by adding layers and make me feel, as well as appear, unnatural.

It's awkward enough when this happens to a woman at the makeup counter of a department store or in a salon or clinic. But when a model is made up wrong, and she knows it, and she has to go before the camera, it is very hard for her to be good for that picture.

I had things to learn, not only about the application of makeup, but about the *use* of it. The commercial use of it.

A camera can be deadly, especially if the lighting is bad (which is sometimes done deliberately to make "before" shots look really terrible so that beautiful pictures can be taken of the "after" look). Cameras do not always tell the truth, but even in excellent close-up work, like beauty shots, lines and flaws are picked up and sometimes even magnified. Remember, most beauty pictures, including those of young, flawless-looking models, are usually retouched and retouched again before they go public. The makeup artist of today, working on the smooth unlined canvas of a youthful face, has almost unlimited freedom to experiment, and today's makeup can be pretty wild. It can also be great fun. But a young face is generally a better playground for abstractions and the glimmer-glitter look so popular today.

I don't think I have to explain to any woman that the cosmetic companies never put out beauty ads that show a natural line or two. A line in your face, even though you have lines from birth, means you are not young. Since the purpose of the ads is to tell us we have to look young and stay young, cosmetics are rarely demonstrated on anyone over thirty—and that's old by commercial beauty standards.

No cosmetics can remove age, but they can make you look more appealing, glamorous, romantic—exactly the *same thing* they do for a young girl. In fact, when the young girl is made up, she usually appears older, while the older woman can appear younger when a makeup job is done correctly.

One of the things I learned from young models and makeup artists is that makeup is fun. It should not be treated as something deadly serious. It should be enjoyed and give pleasure or excitement, bringing the reward of compliments and giving a boost to your feelings about yourself.

I find cosmetics exciting because I'm still curious about the endless possibilities, changes and looks that can be created by an added stroke or line somewhere. I am delighted with myself when I know I've done a good job or created a slightly better look than the time before. When that happens, I go through the day or the modeling job feeling like a million bucks.

Evening makeup can be even more fun than daytime makeup. It demands a different intensity and use of color because of the change in light and clothing. But it should be handled carefully and not overdone just because it's dress-up time. It can be dramatic and beautiful, but should not steal from the main event, which is you.

A woman with delicate, even features can probably get away with using less makeup as she grows older than a woman with stronger, irregular features. But this means she can also play more, exaggerate more and very possibly have more fun.

Through experimentation you will get to know your face, you will get to know makeup and you will be able to bring the two together in a way that will make your beauty more beautiful.

Beauty is not lost with age.

Why should you be?

When Three Simple Steps Aren't Enough

Once you've mastered the basics, you may decide to stop there. But with time and confidence, you may want to experiment with more makeup, as I learned to do. Here are some additional products and techniques you may want to try for a more complex, full facial approach to your makeup.

But first, remember that the most important aid to achieving good makeup is strong clear light—daylight. I often take my tools and a mirror to a window to get light I trust. Even if I don't do the makeup work there, I check what I have done by natural light. Most bathroom and store lighting is very deceiving and can affect your choice of color for bases, blushes and lipsticks. It is hard to get a true reading on colors in artificial light. When you use products repeatedly and know how they look on you, this isn't a problem, but any new color should be checked in daylight.

CREATING A SMOOTH EVEN SKIN TONE

Before you start your makeup, you must prepare the canvas—your skin. It should be scrupulously clean and moisturized. Blot your face with a tissue to remove any excess moisturizer.

When beginning your makeup, first consider the evenness of your facial skin tone. By mid-life, few women have even skin tones (unless they have stayed indoors all their lives). There are three kinds of products to help you cover blemishes and discolored areas: undertone creams, concealers and foundations.

UNDERTONE CREAMS

Undertone creams come in tubes or jars and are used before you apply your foundation base to compensate for ruddy (red tones), sallow (yellow tones) or gray skin. They can also help minimize the amount of base you have to use and allow you to use a lighter textured base. If you have trouble deciding whether or not you need an undertone cream, you probably don't. They are handy, but usually unnecessary, products.

- For too red skin: Use a green or lavender undertone.
- For too yellow skin: Use peach, salmon or beige.
- For too gray skin: Use pale rust to orange or apricot.

When you use an undertone cream, blend it very carefully over the noticeable blotchy areas. You seldom have to use those creams all over your face. Keep the coverage as sheer as possible. Then apply your foundation over it, very lightly.

CONCEALERS

Concealers are used to cover dark circles under your eyes and small blemishes or spots of discoloration on your face. You'll find them in sticks, small pots or tubes with applicators. The latter are the lightest and easiest to use. Choose a shade lighter than your base, and dot it on gently, especially on the skin under the eye, which has no oil glands. The skin under the eye is dry, thin, fragile and can easily stretch. It should never be rubbed. Use the *least* possible amount of concealer here.

To cover eye bags, dot the concealer on the area just *below* the bag and gently blend upward. The idea is not to highlight the puffy area or overload it with makeup. Lighter makeup blended underneath will tend to *lift* the area under the bag, which is in the shadow.

To help reduce lines around the mouth, dot concealer sparingly in the

indentations after applying your moisturizer and then blend carefully with your foundation.

Remember, concealer should be used very sparingly. You do not need a heavy coating to hide flaws. Blend it carefully with your foundation to avoid a buildup in lines or creases.

FOUNDATION

It is very important to find a foundation that is compatible with your skin type as well as your coloring. If a foundation is not right for your skin type, it can change color (turning orangy) or just sit on top of the skin like a layer of paste. Or it may cake or look chalky. If you know your skin type and color as well as what finish you want—matte or dewy—you should be able to find a foundation that gives you a smooth, even, natural-looking skin tone.

Skin types are usually categorized as oily, normal, combination, dry or sensitive. Oily skin generally needs a water-based formula with a sheer or medium consistency. Dry skin needs a creamier formula or an oil-base foundation. Combination skin may need two different types of makeup: creamy on the cheeks and water-based on the T zone (the forehead, nose and chin). Sensitive skin may need a hypoallergenic base with a moist finish.

Testing makeup is really the only way to see if it works for you. Often you can sample makeup at the counter in the cosmetics department. If not, buy the smallest size of a product. After three hours of wear you can see how it reacts to your skin. If it changes color or looks like it is sitting on top of your skin, it's not for you.

Foundations look darker in the bottle than they do on your skin. When testing, if it's not possible to do your whole face, try it on your jawline so you can see the color in relation to both your face and your neck.

Powder matte-finish bases usually show face lines more than other bases, so they don't work well on dry older skin. However, they may be just right for oily skin.

Good application technique makes the difference between a smooth, natural-looking finish and a phony, masklike surface. The best look is as sheer as possible, with some skin showing through. You want the surface to be almost translucent. (Sometimes a tinted moisturizer or a gel bronzer will give you just the coverage you need.) If the look of the foundation seems too heavy on your skin, try diluting the base with just a few drops of moisturizer or water.

You can use your fingers to blend foundation, but I prefer a sponge. It

47

gives just the right coverage. Use a wedge-shaped sponge—very useful for getting into corners—that is slightly damp (not wet). Spread the foundation evenly, blending it carefully with your concealer. Leave no edges or lines, particularly at the neck and hairline.

Allow the base to set for a few minutes before you go on to the next step. Your skin will absorb a certain amount. After waiting, if you feel you have too much on or you can see it on your skin, blot very lightly with a Kleenex to remove the excess. Foundation should be sheer, invisible. If you can see it, you have too much on.

POWDER

Powder will help set the base you have just put on. Many people wait until the last step in their makeup to apply powder, but I believe in doing it earlier. Besides providing a matte finish, it helps keep the blusher you will apply later from disappearing too fast.

I like to apply powder with a large soft sable brush, and I use a loose translucent powder (baby powder will do in a pinch). This gives a softer finish than pressed powder applied with a puff, and it's easier to control the amount you put on. You can use pressed powder *later* for touch-ups and repairs. If you use pressed powder right over your base, you will get a flatter, harder finish than with loose powder. You can use powder without a base, but remember to pick a color that works with your skin color.

First, be sure your foundation base is dry. Then take up a small amount of translucent powder on your brush, shake or tap the brush to get rid of the excess and brush the powder very lightly all over your face, paying particular attention to the T zone area (the forehead, chin and nose). Be sure to powder the tops of your cheekbones also. Remember to use very little powder—you want to keep a moist look. Be careful to brush a second time over face lines to remove any excess that may build up in them, for powder buildup can intensify lines. And keep powder away from your eyes, especially if you wear contact lenses.

Both loose and pressed powders come in shades from ''no color'' to dark brown, with a variety of light and warm tans and beiges in between. Your best all-purpose powder is a translucent no-color shade. If you use a colored powder, it may change the color of your base. You will have to experiment to see if you like the effect.

EYES ARE THE MAIN EVENT ON EVERYONE'S FACE

Study your eyes. See whether you have small or large, wide-set or close-set eyes. The classic Greek ideal is to have one eye's width between your eyes. Notice whether your eyes are deep set or slightly protruding, whether you have narrow lids or wide lids and whether your eyes are set straight in your skull or whether they slant a little up or down. Whatever their nature, the idea is to achieve big bright eyes.

Eye makeup is magic stuff, and magic as we understand it is man creating illusion. In this case, it's woman-made illusion.

49

EYE SHADOW

What kind of eye shadow to choose: You want a soft, subtle, long-lasting color that doesn't call attention to itself. You don't want shadow to collect in the creases of your lids, nor do you want it to show off with glitter and shine. All eye shadows should look as natural as possible, particularly on older lids.

Almost all shiny eye shadows are best on young lids because they usually emphasize the creases. If you get warm and perspire, your shadow can "run" and collect in the folds of the eyelid. Just what you don't want.

Flat shadows are best for eyelids with many creases. Unfortunately, they are out of style right now and difficult to find—just one more example of the lack of concern for the older woman's beauty needs. To get around this problem, I frequently just use a foundation base on my eyelids. It doesn't last as long and needs fresh applications, but while it's on, it works very well—and the colors are neutral and work with any eye color. Try it sometime.

Cream shadows are easier to control than powders, but they also collect in the creases of the eyelids. They last well, although it takes a bit more technique to use them expertly.

If you can't find shadows that don't end up in the creases of your lids, there is a special eye shadow base available that has no oil in it and also a new eyelid cream that keeps shadows on smoothly. Regular base under your eye shadow can help, too.

Eye shadow colors: Light colors help make eyes look larger and more open, while dark colors, though more dramatic, make eyes appear smaller, more closed in, especially if your eye makeup is not expertly applied. Dark colors are better with dark eyes, and very bright colors often steal from the natural color of the eyes themselves, instead of enhancing them. Sand, taupes, soft browns and grays are safe neutral colors for all eyes. They have a more natural look than the brighter colors.

How to use your eye shadow: How you shade your eyes depends on your eye structure and what you want to accomplish. In general, you should cover your eyelids and brow bone up to your eyebrow with a soft tone, then use a slightly darker but complementary color to shade in the indentation at the top of the lid.

If you have small eyes, concentrate your shadow on the far outside corners of the eyes. It helps to use an eyeliner in a dark but harmonious color, making the line darkest at the *outside third* of the lid. Extend the line just a fraction of an inch beyond the eye (but not enough for a slanty-eyed look).

If your eyes are very close set, use eyeliner and shadow only on the outside

third of both the upper and lower lids and brow bone. This will seem to stretch your eyes to the sides of your face.

If your eyes protrude, use a little dark shadow on your lids and line the lower eyelid with a dark eyeliner on the outside and inside edges. This helps create the illusion of deep-set eyes.

EYELINER PENCILS

Eyeliner pencils are very soft and easy to work with, but they also contain grease, which is why they work so smoothly and why they smudge. Any eyeliner that comes in contact with moisturizer or oil under your eyes will run or smudge, as will mascara. To keep this from happening, apply trans-

51

lucent powder with a small brush just under the lower lashes to absorb any residue of oil or moisture.

With eyeliners, you're aiming for a *very soft look*, the softer the better. Pencil eyeliners give the softest line, or they can be made to look soft by gentle blending with a Q-Tip or sponge tip. Lines drawn on with a liquid liner are more definite. I sometimes use both. First I line with a liquid, because I know it will last (and the brush line is fine), then I go over it with a softer color pencil. Mixing two colors sometimes gives you a new soft color that does wonderful things for your eyes. But remember not to make the lines so strong that they overpower your eyes. Work *with* your eye color to encourage its natural color, not diminish it.

To apply eyeliner, follow the natural line of your lids, unless you are making slight adjustments for eye structure (outlined before under eye shadow tips). Lining the inside edge of the top lid—under the lashes—helps make your lashes look thicker. Lining the inside edge of the lower lid with a white or blue pencil brightens your eyes and gets rid of red eye rims (white liner is better for daytime, blue for evening).

Remember, put contact lenses in before doing any work around your eyes. Keep Q-Tips handy to clear up mistakes and to soften hard lines. And if your eyes get irritated, stop using the product—shadow, liner or mascara—that is causing the problem. Switch to one of the many hypoallergenic brands available. And don't ever use other people's eye makeup.

MASCARA

Earlier in this chapter I described basic mascara application. Now you may be ready to experiment with lash-lengtheners or waterproof mascaras. These do wonders to beef up skimpy lashes, but since they have a thicker consistency, they can make your lashes stick together in clumps. This defeats your purpose and creates a heavy spiky look rather than a wonderful flutter of fringe. If your lashes are clumping, immediately comb through them with a fine-tooth mascara comb or a child's toothbrush before the mascara dries.

While all eye makeup will wash off with mild soap and water, waterproof mascaras contain substances to make lashes stiffer and are easier to remove with oil. Look for a commercial mascara remover with oil or use baby oil or vegetable oils.

DYEING YOUR EYELASHES

I have had my eyelashes dyed black on two or three occasions, hoping it would eliminate the need for using mascara. But I was not satisfied with the results, primarily because the dyeing didn't last very long, was reasonably expensive and didn't give the same added thickness to the lashes that mascara does to help frame the eyes beautifully. But if your lashes are very, very pale, you may want to consider this option. Your local beauty salon can give you all of the details.

EYELASH CURLERS

Curled lashes can give your eyes a great wide-open look. Eyelash curlers work best on lashes that are long and fairly straight. The curler will lift them and turn them up. You should use an eyelash curler *before* using mascara, or the curler may stick to your lashes. Place the curler against your upper lid and squeeze your lashes for three seconds—no more. You should get a soft *curve*, not a definite *bend*.

When you apply mascara after the curler, be sure to tilt your chin sharply upward for the upper lashes. Otherwise, your newly curled lashes may leave

53

dots of wet mascara on your brow bone. Wait a minute for the mascara to dry before lowering your head.

Although my eyelashes are quite long, I seldom use an eyelash curler. But I know models who use them faithfully. Up to you.

EYEBROWS EXPRESS

Eyebrows are important to the expression your face wears. They deserve attention and grooming.

Keeping your eyebrows in proportion: Your eyebrows should parallel the natural arch of your eye and should be the right length. Proportions are very important.

In your mind's eye, draw a line from the inside corner of your eye to your eyebrow. That is where your eyebrow should begin. Draw another imaginary line from the tip of your nose to the outside corner of your eye and up to your brow bone. That is where your eyebrow should stop. If eyebrows grow beyond that point, they can give your eyes—and your face—a pulled-down look. Pluck them back.

Grooming your eyebrows: If your eyebrows grow into the space between your eyes, pluck them with slant-edged tweezers. Always pull the hair in the direction it grows. Better yet, have it done professionally.

As you work on your eyebrows, take a toothbrush or an eyebrow brush and brush them up, which will help you see just how they grow. When you've finished grooming them, leave them brushed up a little for a more open expression.

The more you can create the illusion of "up" in everything you do to your face, the better! Your fight is with gravity—learn to keep it at bay for as long as possible.

To even out or darken your brows: Eyebrows that appear to have separations or places where the hair growth is inconsistent—such as when they are turning gray or are just too sparse—can be made to look thicker by using a light beige, taupe or buff-colored pencil (or eye shadow) on them. It should blend in with your natural color—darker colors are too obvious.

A good trick is to fill in the separations or gaps with an eyebrow pencil, using short feathery strokes, then go over the whole eyebrow with a powder shadow. There are shadows specially formulated for eyebrows, or you can use regular eye shadow in a shade that relates to your natural brow.

For too dark brows: Too dark brows can overpower your face. This is particularly true if you have recently lightened your hair or if your hair has turned gray, in which case your brows may have to be lightened or recolored. It's best to have this done professionally. Timing is very important here— you don't want "orange" brows—and a pro will have the know-how you need. After watching your stylist a few times, you may pick up enough expertise to do it yourself. You'll have to lighten your brows as often as you touch up your hair.

There Are No Rules, You Can Try Anything!

As painters constantly experiment, you too can experiment with the tools of makeup. There is no one way to put makeup on your face. If there is one rule, it is only to be sure your makeup is done in good taste and enhances your features and your beauty, but never steals, detracts or overpowers your God-given, unique and beautiful self.

EXPERIMENT WITH YOUR EYES

- Brighten your eyes with a touch of light powder shadow, cream or foundation base on the center of your top eyelid, near the lashes.
- Add sparkle with a tiny dot of white, ivory, cream or yellow at the inside corner of the eye, or at the outside corner if your eyes are too close together.
- Make your soft neutral eyebrow pencil do triple duty: as an eye shadow, an eyeliner and a lip liner.
- Use your eyeliner pencil on your eyebrows when it's the right neutral color.
- Use a regular soft graphite pencil as an eyebrow pencil.

PLAY WITH YOUR LIPS

- Neutralize your natural lip color before putting on lipstick by applying a layer of base or concealer, which also helps to control lipstick. If the foundation is too greasy, dust with a little translucent powder to absorb grease and help keep lipstick on.
- Switch: Brush on lipstick before lip liner. I have often achieved a wonderful-looking mouth this way.
- Create a lip color palette from a small vitamin box with anywhere from two to six compartments. Then you can carry around a variety of lip colors. Cut off pieces of your lipsticks and put them in the compartments. Make one box with daytime colors, another with evening colors. Put some gloss or Vaseline in a compartment. You can even mix colors to get new shades.
- Use a light-colored lipstick as a cream blusher.

SPECIALS FOR YOUR FACE

- For a lighter concealer, use your foundation base.
- Use darker cream or powder blushes as eye shadow.
- Soften your powder or blush color by using translucent powder over or under it.
- Mix blushers for long-lasting color: Use a cream blush under a powder blush.
- Blend two different colors of powder blusher.
- Use a little cream blush on your lips for a soft effect. Powder first, apply a little cream blush, finish with a touch of gloss. It may not last well, but it has a nice effect while it does.

- Use small pill containers (the kind prescriptions come in) to carry loose powder with you.
- To carry your cosmetics, use small clear plastic Baggies. They weigh almost nothing, and you can see what's in them.

You want a beautiful face—

---

be beautifully organized.

Makeup Equipment

The tools you use to make your face beautiful should be kept clean and in working condition.

Pencils should be sharpened so you get the cleanest and best line from them. Get a new sharpener as soon as the blade is dull.

Mascaras should be replaced as soon as they start to thicken, glop or flake.

Brushes should be washed in warm soap and water or with shampoo at regular intervals.

Foundations should be purchased in small sizes. They do dry out, and the oils in some of them can turn rancid. This also allows you to change your makeup from time to time without leaving lots of half-empty bottles.

Whatever you use—*use* it! Get rid of old cosmetics your don't use. Keep your tools at your fingertips, so to speak. Stay organized. Know where your equipment is. If making up becomes inconvenient because you're disorganized, you may also get discouraged.

I keep a certain amount of equipment in the shoulder bag that travels with me every day. There is also equipment in my bathroom, and more that stays in my model's bag, ready to go with me when I have an assignment. I often buy several of a product I use frequently; when I want them, they are right there.

If you work in an office, keep a small plastic zip bag containing your basic necessities in your desk. Your automobile glove compartment, a gym bag or suitcase are other places to stash an emergency fix-up kit.

Take your most beautiful face along with you!

Office Makeup

Looking beautifully groomed and elegantly made up is an important part of your professional image. Office makeup should be as discreet and natural-looking as possible, and it should last through a hectic schedule with minimum touch-ups!

Follow my tips for making your lip and eye makeup last. A lip pencil should be a big help. Learn to use it well. Eye makeup should be very subtle, with a minimum of color on the lids. Go for subtle, smoky shades.

The fluorescent lighting in many offices can do very strange things to makeup color. It's a good idea to keep a folding magnifying mirror in your drawer to check your makeup at your desk, rather than under the lighting in the ladies' room. You may need extra blusher to combat the draining effect of office lighting, and also a brighter shade of lipstick.

When you find out what cosmetics you need to compensate for your office lighting, be sure to keep them in a small cosmetics bag in your drawer for discreet touch-ups. You may also need extra powder for late-afternoon shine, nail polish to touch up chipped nails, and a spray bottle of your favorite, *subtle* cologne to revive you.

Makeup on the Go

Long airplane trips place special demands on your makeup and skin. You want to arrive looking fresh and rested, but there is no more drying atmosphere than the interior of an airplane! If you have a flight of more than two hours, your skin will feel the effects. There are several things you can do to cope.

- Be sure your skin is well moisturized. You may want to skip face makeup and just use moisturizer, so you can reapply it during the trip.
- Take along eye drops and extra contact-lens wetting solution if you wear contacts. Your eyes can get very dry during the trip. You may even want to remove your contacts for the flight.
- Switch to a moisturizing makeup if your normal makeup is water-based.
- If it's possible, remove your makeup during the flight, splash lots of warm water on your face and reapply moisturizer to seal the extra moisture in. You can redo your makeup just before you land.

Hot Weather Tips

Makeup seems to melt right off in hot weather. Yet if you don't want to tan your face (and you really shouldn't), you must protect it. And if you tan your body but *not* your face, you'll want to add some sun-kissed color to your face.

Just recently, cosmetics companies have given us products to save our skin while we enjoy the great outdoors. These new foundations, moisturizers and lip balms have sunscreens to help protect your skin while adding color. Since summer or tropical light is so revealing, you want the sheerest, finest texture possible—just a veil of color. A pale powder blusher over a sunscreen may be all you need, or you may want to dilute your normal makeup with a few drops of water or skin freshener.

Bronzers are another option for faking a tan. Some tend to run when you perspire, so you may want to use them only when you are in dry, air-conditioned places. You can get a very sheer, natural effect if you apply them very lightly.

Other perils of hot weather are streaking (or disappearing) blusher, runny mascara, and eye shadow that collects in the creases of your lids. You can now find water-resistant or waterproof blushers, mascaras and shadows. Some will even last through a swim without smudging or streaking, and you need oil or an oil-based remover to get them off.

For long-lasting summer lip color, prime your lips first with a base or lip balm (preferably one with a sunscreen). Outline your lips with lip liner pencil, then use the *pencil* to fill in the color. It lasts much longer. You can even add a *light* coat of lip gloss for shine.

- A pale blue undertone cream tones down flushed redness or red noses.
- If your cheek color is bleeding or disappearing, double your blushers, using a little powder blusher *over* cream blusher.
- Switch to a water-based foundation in summer, especially if you have *oily* skin.
- Check your makeup colors in the *bright sunlight*. You may need to switch to clearer, brighter colors.

Cold Weather Tips

If you are a skier or enjoy outdoor cold-weather activities, remember to use a sunscreen or cosmetics with sunscreen added. High altitudes mean extra strong ultraviolet rays, and you can get a worse sunburn in very cold weather than in the summer. Use a lip gloss or soothing lip balm under your lip color to prevent chapping.

On Makeovers

It's great fun to find out how someone else would put makeup on your face. I've had the opportunity of being made up by the world's most famous makeup people during photo sessions. Sometimes I was pleased with the results, but sometimes I was not.

We do, however, often get stuck in a makeup rut. And I've discovered how to use some wonderful colors and products from the experts. So if you have a chance to be made up by one of the artists who regularly visit the department store cosmetic areas or if there is a beauty salon in your area with a makeup person, by all means treat yourself to a session with a pro.

But remember one thing: Most of these people are in the business to sell cosmetics. Don't be pressured to buy a lot of products on the spot. Wait until you see the reaction of your family and friends to your new look. And wait a few hours to see how the foundation reacts to your skin, how the colors look under different lights. Too many women go to a makeup expert and walk away with a very expensive bag full of products they never use again.

If you really love your new look, be sure the makeup person shows you exactly how the effect was created, so you can duplicate it yourself at home. And practice!

Sometimes it's fun to let the expert experiment, really go to town with your face. You may discover that gold eye shadow is for you, or find an eyeliner that adds a new sparkle to your eyes. Have the artist create a special evening makeup for you, one that pulls out all the stops with special effects. But keep it in the spirit of fun and discovery. Makeovers should make the most of what you have, not change or disguise the real character in your face.

Makeup for Your Public Life

If your professional life involves appearing before a group, on a stage or dais, you should adjust your makeup accordingly. Strong lights wash out your natural makeup. You should *intensify your face structure* with subtle shading under the cheekbone and along the jawline. Your usual cheek color applied a bit darker than usual should do the trick. You may also want to shade the area around the hairline to give an instant lift to your face.

Project your eyes (you'll want to make eye contact with your audience) with shadow a bit more intense than usual under the brow bone at the top of the lid and add an extra coat of mascara.

Define your mouth with lip pencil and wear a slightly brighter color than usual. Test it under a very bright artificial light to make sure it doesn't fade.

In a Television Studio

Some television studios have wonderful lighting people who literally take years off your face. Others seem intent on focusing on every line. There's not too much you can do except to arrive at the studio early so the lights can be tested if necessary.

Ask ahead if there will be a makeup person on the set. If you have to do your own makeup, practice first under a very bright artificial light (buy a 150-watt bulb if you have no light with over 75 watts). This should give you some idea of how your face fades or washes out under very strong light. Then get a magnifying mirror (the close-up lens of the camera shows everything) and apply your foundation (you may need to go one or two shades darker) and blusher. Remember to avoid a harsh look. You want to intensify and blend well.

Studios in most large cities have makeup people who are there to help you look your best for the camera. You can learn quite a bit from them, so try to pick up a few tips while you're there. They will probably darken your foundation and add a deeper blusher so your face won't wash out under the lights. They'll also intensify your eye and lip makeup.

Makeup for Photography

The average woman is likely to run into two special situations when she'll be photographed: at a public event related to her career or social life or at a snapshot time with the family; and at a formal photography session at a studio, when you need a headshot for professional reasons and it's important to look your best because this is part of your public life (a photo is "forever" and likely to be reviewed in the future).

If you need a formal headshot, choose a photographer who has photographed women in your age group and who understands how to use lighting to show you at your best. Occasionally he or she will take a Polaroid of you first, to check the lighting, and you'll get a preview of the final result.

Eyewear Is a Cosmetic, Too

EYEGLASSES

Eyeglasses came into my life several years ago when I realized I no longer had 20/20 vision. I had always taken good eyesight for granted, and suddenly was confronted with a mind-boggling variety of frames, lenses, contact lenses. I also realized that glasses aren't just necessary evils to help us see. They are the first thing we look at on a person's face, and they have the power of any other feature, particularly since they frame, hide, enhance or distract from the most expressive feature on the face—the eyes.

With eyeglasses, your eyes can suddenly assume a new role. Glasses can give you a look of authority, seriousness, intelligence. A penetrating stare over the top of reading glasses or horn-rims can wield a lot of power. Beautiful lavender or blue shades can hide puffy lids after a late night. Dramatic frames can give instant personality to an otherwise bland face. A meaningful gesture with eyeglass frames can steal a scene.

Glasses can also help compensate for problems in the proportions of your face. Geometric frames add a feeling of structure to a round face, large frames break up the lines of a long face, rounded frames soften an angular face.

With all this going for glasses, isn't it a shame to stick with the same tried-and-true shape for years on end? If glasses are a part of your life, use them to your advantage! Have several pairs (I have three at the moment) for different looks and moods. Think of them as an important part of your eye makeup and bear in mind the following points.

FIT

Go to a good ophthalmologist to have your eyes examined regularly and keep your prescription up to date. Make sure you get the "centers" of your prescription, which are important for accurate placement of the lenses in the frames. An off-center lens can cause headaches and dizziness.

After you have chosen frames, an optician will fill your prescription. Try to choose frames that are easily adjustable. And maybe even get a tiny screw-driver to tighten them from time to time so they won't slide down your nose.

SHAPE

Try on many different pairs until you find the shape that suits you best. Bear in mind that faces with strong bone structure can be softened with graceful curved shapes, while rounded faces can get authority from more geometric, squared-off frames. Also remember: The stronger your prescription, the smaller your frames should be to handle it. Be sure their size is compatible with your prescription. You may also want to consider a veil of subtle color in the lens itself to distract from the thickness of the glass.

COLOR

You have two color options that work to your advantage: the color of the frames and the color of the lens. There's the very subtle, seductive look of shaded lenses, with lighter color at the bottom graduating into a misty eye shadow color at the top. You can choose from mauve, blue, green, topaz, amber and apricot shades. These look particularly glamorous in the new rimless glasses. If your coloring is very light, try transparent, rimless or very narrow metallic frames in pale colors, perhaps with lenses to match. If you have darker coloring, you can take bright colors for fun or warm up your skin with "blusher" shades in apricot tones. Try on a variety of effects, just for fun.

MAKEUP FOR EYEGLASS WEARERS

If you wear glasses, intensify your eye makeup to make your eyes "project" from behind the lenses. Plenty of mascara, a subtle rim of darker eye shadow around the eye and right under the bone will help. Leave a lighter color on the lid. The idea is to create a larger, more defined eye behind the glass.

CONTACT LENSES

Contact lenses give you the freedom to choose if and when you'll wear your glasses. And the freedom to participate in athletic activities that might be impossible or awkward with thick glasses. Today, almost everybody can wear contact lenses. They have been developed to such an extent that you no longer have to worry about the discomfort, the constant blinking, or the complicated sterilization procedures that caused problems when contacts first became available. Bifocal contacts, extended-wear contacts, and implanted contacts for cataract patients are there to solve your vision problems. I urge you to find the best specialist available to fit you for contacts (and beware of companies offering bargain contact lenses). Your eyes are delicate and warrant expert attention.

There's another aspect to contact lenses: changing your eye color. I always dreamed of intense aquamarine eyes. Now I can have them whenever I want just by putting in some tinted soft contact lenses. A fantasy come true! Usually I wear them only for special occasions or when my modeling job requires a dramatic gaze. They're fun, easy to apply and not particularly expensive (about $150).

CLEAR EYES

Ever see a model with red eyes in a photograph? Not on your life. *Eye drops* are a part of my makeup life. If your eyes are continually red, be wary. There may be something internally wrong. If not, try resting for twenty minutes with cotton pads saturated with witch hazel over your eyes. Or try cool tea bags. Cornflower water is a French remedy for tired eyes. It's worth a try if you can find it in your city. (You can also order it from the Caswell-Massey Pharmacy in New York City.)

Looking for beauty?

Remember, you take yourself with you.

You're in Charge

What do I do now that I know all about that equipment models carry in their bags, now that I am comfortable when I sit down before a studio mirror or my own?

I compromise.

I compromise between my early few steps with cosmetics and doing a full makeup job each day. It's simple. It's easy. And it takes a matter of minutes now that I no longer worry about what *they*, cosmetics, will do to me. I know what they do. I've learned I'm in charge of my look, so I'm comfortable using them. And I still enjoy the fun of experimenting.

I think the search for beauty should go on as long as we are alive. When we stop that search, we begin to fade.

No two makeup jobs are ever exactly the same. The differences in my makeup on any given day can be minute and I'm the only one who would notice. I am often told, not asked, that I don't use makeup. I obviously do, but conservatively and carefully. My makeup works for me in a very natural way.

MY DAY FACE

My first move, after finding good light and a mirror, after cleaning and moisturizing my face, is to put in my contact lenses. Then I put some lip cream around the edges of my lips and let it soak in.

I check to see if I have dark circles under my eyes. If I do, I take out a concealer or cover stick and pat some ivory or eggshell-colored cream under my eyes. If I don't, I simply use a light base. I cover not only under my eyes, but also the lids and up to the brow bone. I also use the base down the length of my nose, which has been sunburned so often it seems to be permanently reddish, and on the sides of my nose. I check my forehead to see if I need some base there.

My skin is dry, so I use a cream or liquid base with a damp (not wet) sponge or sometimes just my fingers. The color I use depends on whether I am tan from being in the sun or too pale from being in New York City too long, or some stage in between. I have freckled skin and I make no attempt to hide that fact. Freckles have been natural to me all my life and still are. I also like to leave as much natural light in my skin as possible—because it's natural.

While the base dries or sets, I go to my eyes for the next moves.

I deliberately use base on my eyelids because I like the flat even coverage it gives. Its texture is thin, and I like the light color with my eye color. It also serves as a foundation for a powder eye shadow if I decide to use one. Often I just use a touch of another base, slightly darker in tone, like a suntan color, which is equally good with my blue-green eyes. If I do use an eye shadow, it will be ivory, sand, tan or taupe in color, and with minimum glitter. If I choose to shade, that shadow will be a darker tone of the same family or a complimentary color only a shade or two darker.

With a brown, gray, dark green or dark blue eye pencil, I line my eyelids, top and bottom. I stay with my natural eye lines. I line the top lid, beginning at the inside corner almost underneath those small inside lashes and continuing along the top edge as close into the lashes as possible. I extend that line a fraction further than my own lid line. I leave the bottom line open at the end of my eye deliberately. My eyes are slightly deep set and I think this gives them an open, softer and more fluid look.

I add a coat of black mascara.

While the first coat of mascara is drying, I take an eyebrow brush and brush up my eyebrows. With a taupe or soft gray-brown eyebrow pencil or shadow, I fill in the places that have begun to look spotty because my eyebrows are turning gray. I love having gray hair, but I don't love having gray eyebrows. If I don't have the right pencil or shadow, I use a plain old graphite pencil with soft lead, applying it with short strokes so it doesn't leave hard lines.

My base is long set and has been partially absorbed by my skin. With a powder brush and a little translucent powder, I powder just my cheekbones, down my nose and a touch on the center front of my chin. No more.

The blush I choose will be related to the colors I am wearing that day. As a general rule, my colors are clear ones in the rose and peach families. For evening, I use a deeper or brighter blush from the same families.

With a good medium-sized brush, I cover my cheekbones with powder blush, starting almost directly below the center of my eyes and brushing back along the bones toward the tops of my ears. The blush must be lightly blended as it goes toward my hairline. I continue up my temples right to the corners of my eyes and on to the edges of my brow bone. I give a fast sweep across the top of my forehead close to my hairline. On the lower half of my face, I touch the center of my chin lightly and then run the brush along the underside edge of my jawbone, barely touching it. If I have done all this well, my face looks balanced and has a warm glow. It should not look as if I have used blush on my face.

Second coat of mascara.

I pat a little base on my lips, and with a soft-colored lip pencil outline my lips, widening the corners just a fraction. I brush on lipstick that works with my clothing and the blush. A little powder and another coat of lipstick— sometimes. Other times, I just leave it after the first coat and repair it during the day.

If I haven't been working in daylight, I go to the window and check what I have done. If I think my eyes should look brighter, I might add a spot of white or yellow or ivory at the center of my eyelid, close to the lashes. This acts like a miniature spotlight, picking up color and brightening the eyes. Keep it soft though.

MY EVENING FACE

If I am going out in the evening and do not have the luxury of leisure time to bathe and do a new evening face, I make do by redoing.

I rub my face with a tissue, pat it with a damp washcloth and put on fresh moisturizer that is very light in texture and will absorb quickly. I repeat what I did in the morning, using deeper colors of blusher and eye shadow. I comb through my eyelashes, put on fresh mascara and touch up my eyeliner if necessary. The only new addition is a little light ivory or cream highlighter on my brow bone and on my cheekbones close to my eyes. A little light eye shadow can do the same job.

When I have the time to do a fresh makeup job on myself for an evening out, I add a full base instead of a partial one and I brush a very fine, barely pink powder lightly all over my face, which gives it a lovely warm and romantic evening look. Other than that, I do everything else just the same, except to use slightly more intense colors for the night light.

In the last ten years, I have put on makeup in cabs careening around New York City, in lurching vans going to a modeling location, in airplanes, on beaches and in windswept fields, on sidewalks, in poorly lit rooms, sitting on studio floors, somebody's lawn, or benches and behind bushes in Central Park.

I consider makeup an art, a necessary art today, and I like the ongoing challenge to be creative it presents. Creative with and for myself—but always with the added hope that it will give pleasure to those around me who care and like me, and even to those I don't know who will see me.

I take myself with me wherever I go, and I like to do that beautifully.

BEAUTIFUL HAIR, BEAUTIFU'L YOU

> If you think there is only
>
> one age to be beautiful—
>
> that's an opinion, not a fact.
>
> Advertising's opinion.

IS there anything that pleases, upsets, concerns, bothers, delights, frustrates and consumes our attention more than our hair? I don't think so. It's a well-known fact in the cosmetics business that more money is spent on hair and hair products than on anything else. Whatever type of hair has been genetically given to us, we usually want the opposite.

I am no exception. My hair is coarse, wavy, curly, thick and dry, and while I like its thick and heavy qualities, I would rather have it straight, soft and shiny. Hair that I could grow long. Very long. I want to be able to swish it around suggestively, pull it back, wear it up and make myself into many different types—all with my hair.

One of my earliest memories as a child was of people touching my hair and saying things like: "Oh, what beautiful curls." And then, more often than not, someone would recite the child's verse:

There was a little girl
Who had a little curl
Right in the middle of her forehead;
And when she was good
She was very, very good,
But when she was bad she was horrid.

My family learned to recite this to me when I was not behaving properly, and I learned to associate curly hair with "horrid."

By 1975, I had begun to model. Within two years I had my hair cut off, as short as it is today. I gave up all dyeing, streaking and straightening and I let it be—natural. I was finally ready to work with it instead of against it. It was a fairly risky decision at that time because I was told repeatedly that I would never work if I cut my hair so short. And then I let it go gray and was told that I would *absolutely* never work. Hiding one's age was essential, particularly in the glamorous world of modeling. Modeling, after all, was only conceivable if you were young. If I wanted to work, even occasionally, I must do everything I could to look young and lie about my age.

So much for paying attention to advertising. The truth is, I would never have worked if I had not done what I did. The benefit was mine all the way around. I did what was right for me.

But I did go through stages. I had to conform until I was ready not to and was ready to do what suited me.

How It Grows . . . or Doesn't Grow!

Our hair literally grows out of our skin, just as our fingernails and toenails do, and all are made up of the same properties. Hair is approximately 95 percent protein and keratin and the remainder is pure moisture, which explains why hair responds to moisture in the air or lack of it. Hair, like your skin, loses its moisture.

Our hair grows in layers, and each strand is covered by a sheath called the cuticle, which acts like a shield to protect it. Hair grows at the rate of one quarter inch per month. It grows faster in the summer, and rests in between spurts of growth. All growth goes on only at the root of the hair, which is out of sight in the hair follicle. The hair follicles on our scalp are part of our skin, as are those on our body. When a hair emerges from a skin follicle, it is technically considered dead.

Hair is at its strongest when we are nineteen or twenty years old. After that, it begins, imperceptibly, to grow weaker. Any hair follicle can reach a point when it will no longer create a new strand, and thus our hair begins a thinning process.

Hair follicles give up for many reasons: heredity, pollution, poor treatment that damages the scalp, inadequate blood circulation to the head, excessive oiliness—known as seborrhea—that blocks the hair follicle, poor nutrition, stress and age. Nutrition is not a major cause of hair loss unless you have really starved your body of protein, which could then affect the protein content of your hair. If your system is starved for protein, hair growth will slow down but will pick up again when protein is restored to your body.

Stress is considered a major cause of thinning hair in women. Prolonged stress affects the nervous system, and when your body stays in a state of extreme tension, the blood flow to your head is restricted. This keeps your scalp and hair follicles from supplying nourishment to the growing hair.

Eighty percent of all women begin to lose some hair either at the onset of or throughout menopause. Most of this hair loss is at the hairline or at the top of the head or scalp. Some women lose as much as 25 or 30 percent of their hair at this time. Although a lot of hair will still be left, it will be permanently thinner.

Another cause of temporary hair thinning is just plain abuse. Beauty abuse. The protective cuticle of our hair is not made of steel. It can be damaged far more easily than most people realize, and when it is injured—cracked or stripped—your hair changes. Commercially speaking, it is damaged, wounded hair. Too much sun, sharp narrow-tooth combs, spiky hard nylon hairbrushes, swimming pools loaded with chemicals, blow-drying at too high a temperature and holding the dryer too close to your head, teasing, bleaching, dyeing, straightening, using overly alkaline shampoos (your hair and skin are more acidic than alkaline), hard scratching and hard rubbing with towels when hair is wet—all can damage the protective hair cuticle.

Like anything in nature, the more you *improperly* interfere by imposing things foreign on your hair, the more you risk damaging it. When your hair is wounded severely enough, it can break, and there is still no known way to restore strength to weakened and damaged hair. It can only be pampered and protected by conditioners and allowed to restore itself to its natural state. The best treatments available won't make your hair more beautiful than it was when nature gave it to you in the first place, before you interfered.

The quality and quantity of your hair and its thickness or thinness have to do with your genetic inheritance, just like your hair color. Some disagree about whether blondes or brunettes have the greatest number of hairs on their heads, but it is agreed that redheads have the fewest. Most women have about a hundred thousand hairs on their scalp. As you age, so does your skin and hair. The melanin that controls their color fades. When it is completely gone from your hair, you have white hair.

I think there is little doubt that the need to treat your hair carefully and tenderly becomes much greater from mid-life on, though obviously the better you have treated your hair since the beginning of your life, the better your hair has probably served you.

And your hair should serve you—not the other way around.

Understanding Your Hair

Before you decide how to wear your hair, you need to understand what type it is, its composition or texture and how it behaves naturally. Yes, you may have been looking at your hair all your life, but you may still not understand it!

Since your hair is an outgrowth of your skin, it should get the same attention. Just as you have normal, dry or oily skin, so do you have normal, dry or oily hair.

DRY HAIR

Dry hair often goes with dry skin and scalp. The dryness is caused by not having enough natural oil coating the hair shaft to keep it supple or lubricated. If your scalp is dry and flaky, it probably is not dandruff but dermatitis, an irritation that can be controlled by shampoos. As we grow older, those glands that secrete the needed oil slow down.

Dry hair can be fine and hard to control, flying about in all directions. It can also be coarse and wiry, thick or thin, wavy or straight. Whichever combination you have, dry hair needs a regular conditioner, just as dry skin needs moisturizing.

OILY HAIR

Oily hair also comes with any combination of characteristics: curly or straight, fine or coarse, thick or thin. It can be prone to dandruff problems if excess oil causes clogging at the hair follicle and a buildup of scaling. Dandruff is considered a minor disease for which there is no cure but excellent control.

Oily hair needs frequent cleansing, usually daily. You may also help its condition by cutting fats and oils from your diet. The less oil going into your system, the better for your health in general, but specifically for your overly oily hair and scalp.

NORMAL HAIR

Normal hair is just-right hair—neither too oily nor too dry. It has good texture, it's easy to work with and it can go a few days between shampoos. It is balanced.

YOUR SCALP CONDITION

Whatever kind of hair you have, your scalp should be kept in the best possible condition at all times. If you have extreme problems with a dry or an oily scalp that you can't bring under control by using shampoos with medicated formulas for these conditions, you should consult either a dermatologist (skin specialist) or a trichologist (hair specialist).

Scalp grooming is really part of hair grooming. Keeping a clean and healthy scalp so that the skin can function normally is your first step to having healthy hair.

And healthy hair is *beautiful hair.*

Your Shampoo

People with normal or dry hair can use the same shampoos. When your hair is very dry, you should lather it only once to leave some of your natural oil in the hair. You should also dilute your shampoo with an equal amount of water for a gentler treatment.

Oily or greasy hair needs daily shampooing with products made specifically for that type of hair. Find those that keep the acid/alkaline balance of your hair at the ideal level. These are called P-balanced shampoos and will improve and strengthen the hair shafts as well as add shine and control. They are labeled according to hair condition, so you can find one specifically for your hair type.

After shampooing your hair, rinse thoroughly. A cool to cold final rinse will add more shine to your hair by closing the cuticle. Try it!

Wet hair should first be wrapped or patted with a towel. You may then comb it with a wide-toothed comb that has rounded teeth, starting at the bottom and gently working your way up the hair shafts, being careful not to stretch and strain them by yanking and pulling.

Conditioners: For Sexy Hair at Any Age

What is sexy hair? It is shiny, soft, touchable hair. It looks healthy, alive. It moves. It is one of the greatest beauty assets a woman can have. And every woman *can* have sexy hair. It's a matter of getting it in the best condition possible.

What sexy hair is not: rigid, tight, sprayed, overteased. The color is flat, false, at odds with your skin tone. It is so styled that it doesn't tempt a man to touch it.

Shiny, healthy hair is yours for the caring. First, you or your hairstylist must accurately assess its condition. Look at your hair in bright sunlight. Does it shine? Are the ends split? Is the color uniform from the ends to the roots, or are the roots a brassier, dried-out version of the original shade?

Most of the problems that come from overtreating, sun damage and over-processing can be improved almost miraculously with the right conditioner. What you see in dry, flat, lifeless hair is the ragged surface of the mistreated strand itself, multiplied thousands of times. When that surface is smoothed down and coated with a good conditioner (like giving your nails a gloss of shiny enamel), the hair springs to life again.

When you use chemical processes such as dyeing or permanent waving, conditioners must become a part of your life. It's a trade-off you must make. Your hairdresser is the best guide. Ask which products he or she uses and get them in a beauty-salon supplier's store if necessary. There are conditioners to moisturize, add body, or plump up very fine hair to make it look thicker.

Normal hair may not really need a conditioner, but it is useful to add protection. Dry hair, on the other hand, should be conditioned every time you wash it. Oily hair needs a nonoily conditioner, maybe just a rinse to detangle hair strands. Black people have very delicate hair and often need a conditioner high in protein to strengthen and protect it.

If your hair is seriously damaged, you may need deep-conditioning treatments. You can buy products or packs for deep-conditioning hair anywhere, but one of the most commonly used treatments is oil—vegetable oil, olive oil, almond oil, even mayonnaise—rubbed into the hair and scalp and then wrapped in hot towels, plastic wrap or a shower cap and heated under an electric hood or hair dryer. Leave it on for twenty minutes to a half hour or longer if possible. You will need to rinse your hair several times to get the oil out, but the shine is worth it.

There are also the old standby highlighters that contain no dyes and make the hair appear shinier: lemon juice, chamomile, rosemary, vinegar, beer and henna.

Here are some ways to help your conditioner do its best work.

- Leave it on your freshly shampooed hair long enough. If you rinse it out too soon, you won't get the full benefit. The hair needs at least twenty minutes to absorb the product.
- If you color your hair, have a permanent or have sun-damaged hair, condition with a protein-based conditioner every time you shampoo. You must give back to the hair what has been taken away.
- Harsh weather can dry hair out, damage the cuticle and fade color. So if you are in strong sunlight or high winds, condition your hair as soon as possible. Or slather conditioner on your hair before you go outside. The heat from strong sunlight at the beach or on the tennis court can help the conditioner penetrate.
- Dilute your shampoo with an equal amount of water. It's gentler on the hair (and your shampoo will last much longer).
- If you take saunas or steam baths, put conditioner on your hair first. The heat will help it penetrate.
- Protect your hair from the sun. Sun not only can dry out hair, but can also change its color. You may like a few sun streaks, but not the greenish or orangy cast that appears when the sun attacks your artificial hair color. There are sunscreens for hair available now—well worth tracking down if you have color-processed hair.
- Pool chemicals are other natural enemies of your hair. You can protect your hair against dehydration and chemical damage by combing a deep conditioner through it before you swim and rinsing it in the shower immediately after leaving the pool. To protect your color, however, it's best to wear a swim cap.
- Check the ingredients in all conditioners for possible irritants. Your skin and hair are of the same substance. What irritates your facial skin can also irritate your scalp.

Coloring Your Hair

Treating your hair with care and knowledge is essential as you grow older, particularly because your hair does not have the same strength it had when you were twenty. You want know-how, not guesswork, from either yourself or a professional.

I speak from the heart. Once upon a time, when I was in my mid-thirties, I went to a beauty salon I had never been to before. It had an excellent reputation in a major New England city. I wanted color. I had dyed my hair before and, while it was dry as usual, it was generally in very good condition. Nothing to worry about. The day was my wedding anniversary. My husband, Bill, was flying in that evening and we were going to have a special dinner together.

At the beauty salon, I was introduced to the man who would do the color work. I was told he was new, but that he had spectacular references. I handed myself over to him without a murmur, in full confidence. A couple of hours later, I looked in the mirror at someone I had never seen before. My hair was dark black and I had aged an instant ten years because of it. Aged badly. It was harsh, hard and totally unsuitable for me.

So much for my anniversary dinner with Bill. Even a lovely diamond pin and assurance that it wasn't really as terrible as I knew it was did not stop the tears that night or for most of the next week. I tried to get it lightened, I got haircuts, and it only got worse.

Neither the beauty parlor nor I had asked the man who did the color the right questions about how well trained he was. Know whom you are dealing with and what his or her experience has been.

Beautiful, richly colored hair is an attainable asset. If you don't like your natural hair color, there is no reason to live with it. What is important is that the color you choose be as natural as possible. And today, that translates into hair that is a blend of many different shades. Not an easy effect for the home colorist to achieve. Many, many women now color their hair at home with varying degrees of success. What I see most is a flat, one-color effect that is harsh on the skin and takes a great deal of care and maintenance to keep in good condition.

Before you do a radical color change on your hair, consider highlighting. A brunette can become a much more natural-looking blonde by coloring many but not all strands of hair, perhaps concentrating the lighter colors near her face and shading back to more of her natural color. It takes an expert to judge the exact placement of the strands. But since the final effect is more "tortoiseshell" than all-over color, you'll need touch-ups less frequently.

Here are some things to remember about color:

- For the most natural color, more than one shade in the same color range should be used, with streaking, tipping, staining and shading effects.
- Thin hair looks thicker when shaded or highlighted with a color only a tone or two lighter than the original shade.
- Light hair looks thicker than dark hair.
- Brows complement your new hair color when they are the same color or a shade or two lighter.
- Lighter hair at the center front can add length to a wide face.
- Lighter hair at the sides can add width to a long face.
- Waves of darker hair around the face can help soften the angles of a square face.
- Warm golden tones will pick up ash-brown hair.
- Red tones can brighten pale skin.
- Take the yellow out of gray hair with a special toner, not a blue rinse!
- The straighter your hair, the more a color change will show up (and so will the slightest mistake). Dramatic effects or strong color contrasts work best on curly hair.
- The more often a lightener is used on your hair, the more porous the hair becomes. It can also get delicate and brittle. Always use extra conditioning on the ends when you touch up your color, to avert damage and to be sure your color is distributed evenly (porous untreated ends will absorb more color than the roots).
- If your hair begins to get stretchy when washed, overly elastic or inordinately dry, or starts to coil into snarls and kinks in unusual ways, you are overcooked with chemicals. Your hair needs an immediate rest and the best conditioning help you can give it.

COLORING NATURALLY

Throughout time, women have colored and toned their hair with available natural sources: vegetables, fruits, nuts, berries, herbs, grapes (red wine), beets, rhubarb, carrots, walnuts, tea, coffee and, for thousands of years, henna. Henna is a shrub found in India, Iran, the Levant and on the northern coast of Africa and is sometimes referred to as an herb, and sometimes as a vegetable. The dye it yields—which comes in reddish, dark or neutral colors— is particularly good for brunettes, redheads and black hair. By coating the hair strands, it adds color, condition and a beautiful shine. The color and shine last for several months. Henna doesn't hide gray, however, and can turn it a rather unflattering shade of orange or red, so be sure to have a color test first. It is best to find a hairdresser who has had a good deal of experience with the different shades of henna and henna products.

PERMANENT COLORS

Permanent hair-coloring processes will actually chemically alter your hair structure. Again, there is a trade-off involved. Because your hair is made more porous by a peroxide solution, it will accept the new color. But you will have to step up your conditioning to strengthen the treated hair strands. If you use a permanent hair color at home, stay within a shade or two of your natural color. Don't try to go from black to blonde. You will see new body and shine in your hair, especially if it is fine, limp or dull, because the coloring process will coat the hairs.

SEMI-PERMANENT COLOR

Semi-permanent coloring involves no stripping agents or chemicals. The color thus penetrates the hair shaft, but does not seal or bond into the hair.

Semi-permanent colors give new tone to the hair, but they do not lighten it. They come combined with shampoos and conditioners or as rinses. The color will last about four weeks, fading out gradually. Semi-permanent colors also thicken or add body to fine and porous hair and jazz up color, particularly when your own hair color looks dull.

TEMPORARY COLOR

Temporary-color products are water soluble and last only from shampoo to shampoo. They are the mildest coloring agents available. You apply them with a cotton ball on damp hair after a shampoo, working from the roots outward. Or you can find them in foam versions, like a mousse, to apply to a section of your hair for a special effect. This is a good way to preview a slight color change or some new highlights. Temporary color alters the tone of your hair just a bit, tones down a color or temporarily blends in unwanted white or gray hair. Remember, it is temporary and water soluble. The color can come off on your pillow at night, after swimming or if you get caught in a heavy rainstorm.

STREAKING

Streaking involves bleaching, unless you buy products that you can "paint" on yourself for temporary results. Streaking has to be very well done to look natural, so I strongly advise seeing an expert colorist. You don't want to come out with a "striped" head! The colorist will strip the color from sections of your hair and then apply toners to give them a natural, sun-lightened effect. Well done, streaking is a good solution for adding a blonde look to your hair without having to constantly retouch or have roots show. The process needs repeating every few months.

On Keeping That Gray!

Skin and hair are one. They are the same fabric, and, like any fabric, their texture and color harmonize to make a statement. Our skin and hair are constantly changing, and you should remember that when you decide you want to use color. When does anyone decide that? Really at almost any age today, and it can be for one or a dozen different reasons. But by mid-life, one of the major reasons you might decide to color is because you are getting gray. Your hair and skin are slowly losing pigment. They are changing.

Trying to duplicate or re-create the exact color your hair once was may not be the best for you now because your skin tone has probably changed, too. Consider this when you think about hair color changes.

When gray shows up, many people can't believe it's really there. The timing of its appearance is different for everyone and is determined by heredity.

If gray hair is reported to be drier hair, it is only because the oil glands in the scalp have slowed down and are not producing the same amount of oil. This happens whether or not your hair turns gray and has nothing to do with the color.

Gray hair is no more of a problem than other "color" hair unless you think it is, and we have certainly learned to think it is in the last twenty-five years. When gray or white hair reaches the stage where it becomes beautiful and flattering, working with your skin coloring and eye coloring, it can become *youthful*, setting off your natural coloring with a brightness and a vibrancy that darker colors, which may have worked for you in the past, no longer do. Now, since your skin color has changed, these darker colors overshadow your face, stealing from it instead of complementing it with light. Light in every sense of the word.

Gray or partially gray hair can be highlighted very naturally by using a temporary color (slightly lighter than your original color) on the natural frost you've acquired. I've said it before and I'll repeat: *Never go darker as you get older, go lighter.* Lighter hair is softer with the lines on your face and your changing skin color. Gray hair does not have to be old yellow or blue at any time, no matter what color you use, unless for some reason you want those shades or they work with your skin tones.

I made the decision to "go gray," as they say, after I had been modeling for two years. I found it was an expensive proposition to keep getting color and then having it trimmed off every three to four weeks. When I let nature have her way, she won. She should have. She was right. But I was anxious when I was told that I probably would not be able to continue modeling with gray hair, that there were not calls for gray-haired women. Finally, I decided that since I worked so little anyway I had nothing to lose. I won. I worked more.

Mid-life looks like mid-life. Youth looks like youth. What we have forgotten is that mid-life looks fantastic. I was in mid-life, and the best way to say it was to be me. I have seen women with gray hair who are very beautiful, more beautiful with it than without it. I was ready for my next look. Gray is beautiful.

Any age means alive.

Don't betray life.

Always find your beauty.

There'll Be Some Changes Made . . .

Don't change your hairstyle if you know:

- The proportions of your hair are correct for your head and face.
- Your features are properly and beautifully flattered.
- Your color is best for your skin tones.
- You can manage your style yourself, comfortably, and can maintain the look you like.

Some women decide to go for drastic change in their hair right after a crisis in their lives: divorce, a period of inner turmoil, a declaration of independence.

Suddenly there's a desire to get in touch with what's new and modern, and that is translated into changing hair color, look or length. (It is said that the first thing a *man* does after a divorce is have his hair "styled" instead of going to his usual barber!)

A new hairstyle gives you a change of look but is not always a change for the better. Change for its own sake is not the answer. You want a lift, not the letdown of looking worse than before. That's why it's especially important for you to find the best stylist you can (and for heaven's sake, don't go hacking at your hair yourself or have a friend or neighbor color it for you).

Don't take things out on your hair. Do keep an open mind and place confidence in your stylist. Changing your hairstyle just to change it is valuable only if it's an improvement and the change is "you." Every woman understands that phrase.

Yes, it can be risky. But if the way you wear your hair can be improved, it is better to take the risk than to stay stuck with an outmoded and possibly aging hairdo, one that is inappropriate like the old beehive or an overly bouffant, laquered-stiff and unnatural style that never moves, making you self-conscious of your every motion because you are afraid it will come "unglued." Or the cute hairdo that may have been adorable at some early tender age, like wearing barrettes or keeping it too long and loose when your face and maybe your body proportions have changed. And, last but not least, the perm.

The Perm. I'm talking about the frizzy perm that millions upon millions of middle-aged women wear. The safe perm. The perm of least resistance. The perm that sometimes three generations of a family may be wearing. The perm that seems to say: I've had it; I'm not going to bother about myself anymore. The perm that consigns you to age, that says to hell with it all, who cares, I'm not beautiful.

I'm not saying this perm is never good or appropriate. But it can't be the answer for so many women. I know there are good perms and bad perms and I understand that you may not have an expert around the corner. Or, if you do, the only thing he or she may be expert at is giving *one* kind of permanent. I have traveled the country extensively in the last few years and I swear I sometimes think the women in entire communities wear the exact same permanent, as though everyone is afraid she won't look like everyone else. It's a hair-perm uniform.

A whole town? Lots and lots of whole towns?

The very fact that women are frequently so quick to relinquish what they claim is most important to them, their unique individuality, their look, demonstrates how fragile are our feelings about our looks, our beauty. At any age. Think of the sixties. Hair was life. Identity. Practically all the kids and lots of adults of both sexes madly grew their hair. They all began to look alike. At the same time, they loudly proclaimed their individuality. Confusing? I think so.

Forcing a new hairstyle, one you may have seen on someone else and think you want because you like it on her, is only reasonable if you have similar type hair, head shape, features, body structure and coloring. You *must* consider all of yourself, not just your head. Trying to superimpose a look where it may not belong is no improvement for you.

Hair changes do not have to be wildly dramatic or major. Sometimes something as minor as changing your part or the direction you comb your hair, cutting it an inch or two longer or shorter, going from straight to curly or wavy or from frizzy to smooth, changing the color tone, shine, or texture can give positive improvement and, subtle or otherwise, a change in your look.

Hair Style *Is* a Good Haircut

I think the single most important hair consideration for any woman is her haircut— and the way she wears it. Haircuts can be dramatic. Wonderfully dramatic. They can change not only your look, but your outlook.

A good haircut is style. It is fundamental to whatever else you do to your hair. *When your face-to-hair proportions are out of balance, your face will lose every time to what is going on with your hair.* The idea is to find the correct working balance. That has everything to do with style, just as it does in makeup and clothing.

I know if I didn't get a good haircut—no, an excellent haircut—my hair would quickly be a nondescript mass of kinks and waves with no style. I seek out haircutters, professionals who take pride in their artistry and ability to cut hair. Professionals who know how to cut *with* my waves and curls and not work against them. This creates control as well as style. For women with straight hair, the cut is even more crucial. Every snip shows.

I have a relatively small head and facial structure. Today, my face is thinner than when I was in my twenties and thirties. I know that if I tried to grow my hair again to play out my youthful hair fantasy, my features would soon be lost or overwhelmed by too much hair. I sometimes err to the other extreme and let it be cut a little too short. I also know I could allow it to grow somewhat longer than it is today and it would still work for me. I look for balance with every hair trim.

If you are not getting a good haircut, stop spending your money on other things related to your hair and put it toward the best haircut you can find, even if you have to travel a distance to get it.

Whatever is written about different hairstyles and how hair may best be worn with different face and head shapes and hair textures, there are always exceptions. I don't know anyone, including the hair experts, who can cover all the possible exceptions. Remember, each one of us is unique. Remember, too, that nothing is written in stone. Stay flexible in your thinking about everything, including your hair.

In general, I think today's shorter styles are wonderful for the mid-life woman. They have an upbeat look that is natural and fresh. This is important as we grow older. Gravity is doing its damnedest to pull everything down, and we have to learn to work in the opposite direction. Think up, stand up straight, and wear a hairstyle that gives your face an up look.

Hair that is worn loose and long, straight down, conspires to emphasize the down lines in the face when we are older. Short hairstyles are more open and create an up look. Obviously, long hair worn up and handled beautifully can create the same feeling as short hair.

Hair that is too dark for your skin tone will make your face look hard and can age even a youthful face, but it is particularly hard on an older face. And if your hair is bushy, shapeless and frizzy, that will add years.

When getting your hair cut, remember:

- Tall, slender women look more attractive with longer hair than short, heavy women do.
- Hair that is thick and straight is best with a blunt cut, as is thin hair.
- Curly hair is best worn short. It can be cut short all over the head or a little longer in a layered or blunt cut. Curly hair should not be thinned.
- Baby-fine hair is better short, about chin length, as it tends to get scraggly if it is long. Fine hair should be blunt cut, very skillfully—every slip of the scissors shows!

FOR VERY THIN HAIR

If your hair is so thin that your scalp shows through, it sometimes helps to change your part. Try lowering it or combing your hair forward instead of to the side, creating a frame around your face. Consider bangs worn straight across your forehead or brushed to one side. If your hair is very dark, try lightening it or letting it get naturally light, gray or white. Light hair blends with the scalp better and minimizes the look of thin hair.

A HAIRCUT THAT WORKS NOW . . . AND LATER

One haircut that works especially well today is the bob. It is not new (remember the Dutch bob?). The latest variation is fresh, youthful, will give you a variety of different looks and works with almost any type and texture of hair. You do need a good blunt cut that goes straight across the ends of the hair shafts. This cut adds body to the hair.

You can wear a bob in several lengths, from just below the ear to just above the shoulders. It can be long enough to work with combs pulled back at the temples, a headband, or even an upsweep. Left alone, it is simple, clean-looking and elegant. It involves minimum setting—many women can just comb it into place after washing and conditioning, let it self-dry or blow-dry it, and push it into shape with their fingers and maybe a bit of gel or hair-styling mousse.

Finding the Hairstylist Who Is Right for You

Finding a stylist who understands your hair and will give you a good cut that takes the natural characteristics of your hair into account and is suited to your way of life is one of the best and nicest things you can do for yourself. But it takes thought on your part and a bit of investigation.

I wouldn't advise you to just walk into a salon and take your chances. If you do, you risk getting the salon's mass-produced haircut of the day, getting rushed through your appointment, getting the salon's least booked (and least skillful) stylist and maybe getting hustled into a costly treatment, color change or permanent you don't want or need.

So, instead of putting your hair and your looks in the hands of the stylist, think of working *with* him or her as a partner. There must be communication and understanding for you to get what you really need and for the stylist to be satisfied, really interested in helping you.

Though a good stylist is trained to do almost any hairstyle, most salons have a special philosophy or an age group they cater to. Some are known for treatments, some for color, some are very avant-garde, some have blaring

disco music, some do the same rigid hairstyles they've been doing for years. First find out the general look of the salon's customer. Go there for a small service, like a manicure or a wash and set. Look at the work being done by different stylists and see which one you like. If the personnel are rude, if your appointment is delayed unduly, if you feel rushed, go elsewhere. *A beauty salon visit should be a pampering experience, never an ordeal.*

Another good way to find a stylist—perhaps the best—is by recommendation. Ask anyone whose hair you admire where she gets it done. Even though her look might not suit you, a good-looking hairstyle can put you on the trail of a talented haircutter.

Next, meet the stylist *before* you make an appointment to get your hair cut. Ask for a ten-minute consultation in advance. A good stylist will come up with several ideas for improving your looks. This also gives him or her a chance to see you face to face in street clothes. This is very important because your hair must relate to how you dress and your overall proportions. Wear your regular street clothes and makeup—don't go in looking too casual. If the stylist is too busy to see you, perhaps he or she is also too busy to give you the attention you deserve.

During your consultation, get some idea of how much the total service will cost, so you have no surprises when the final bill comes. Good hairstylists, especially in major cities, are expensive but worth it. When your hair looks terrific, everything you wear gets a lift. If your hair is wrong, it can throw off the most chic, expensive outfit. It's worth the investment. And it's worth some time and thought on your part to get the right person—you're building one of the most important relationships in your beauty life.

Come armed with an overall knowledge of your hair and how it behaves. Tell your stylist how much time you can devote to maintaining the style. If you have no time for complicated setting or maintenance routines, if you swim every other day, if you can't handle a blow dryer, tell the stylist! It also helps to bring a visual point of reference, like a magazine photo of a style you like. However, don't expect to look exactly like the photo: Your hair or face shape may not work with that particular style.

When you find a stylist you like, respect and feel comfortable with, book your first appointment on a day and at a time when the salon is not too busy. Mondays or Tuesdays are good days. Try to be the first in the morning. You want the stylist to be unhurried and to concentrate on you without a backup of customers.

Give the stylist direction, but don't stifle creativity. Your stylist may see wonderful possibilities in your hair that you never dreamed of. So, before vetoing a new or radical idea, use the stylist's creativity to your advantage. Listen to the expert, then think it over and make your own decision.

Bear in mind that one salon may not do everything well. Good cutters are not necessarily good colorists. You may have to go to one place for cutting, another for color. Hair coloring is a very special talent, and it's worthwhile looking for the best available. However, if you decide to have a permanent, do it at the same place where your hair is cut so the permist and your haircutter can work together. The cut and the curl must harmonize.

After the cut and styling, be sure to ask how to maintain the style. Find out what products were used—if there were mousses, gels, sprays to give your hair body or volume. Get as many maintenance tips from your stylist as you can.

If you don't like the cut, say so immediately. It may be simply a matter of adjusting the styling. Or your eye may not be adjusted to the change. But even a top haircutter can't satisfy everybody. If you are truly unhappy, chances are the salon will remedy the situation. Remember, the salon wants you as a steady client.

Working with Your Hair: The Basic Tools You Need

Beside doing the absolute most for your looks, your hairstyle should be easy to maintain at home. A great cut almost always takes care of itself. You can tell if you have one by just washing your hair and letting it dry naturally. Then shake your head vigorously. Your hair should fall into a definite shape that complements your face. With just a few strokes of a brush, you should be able to face the world with a good, if casual, look. Your styling may not be as finished or polished as you would like, but the basic shape should be there. That's a good cut.

If you feel dependent on a blow dryer, a hot comb or electric rollers; if you feel you absolutely have to have a wash and set every week; if after you wash your hair it hangs in no particular shape or looks ragged, your basic cut is to blame. Also take into consideration the condition of your hair. It should be in the best condition possible to show off the cut to good advantage. If during that basic "shake" your hair seems frizzy and out of control, you may need a good conditioner.

To style your hair, you first need the obvious: a comb and a brush. Choose those that treat the hair very gently. Combs with widely spaced round teeth are easiest on the hair. So are brushes that have bristles with rounded ends. A brush with wide-spaced rounded bristles and a ventilated open base can shorten your blow-drying time and add volume to your hair. If these are not available in your drugstore, track down a beauty supply store that sells to salons. Those brushes with close-set bristles, also on a flexible base, are good for smooth style.

The hand-held dryer is an important styling tool when properly used. Choose a low setting and keep the dryer moving, held about six inches away from the hair. Then section your hair with a wide-tooth comb into side, back, top and top front. Work around the head, section by section, drying the top last. Always keep the dryer moving, and blow against the direction of your hair growth for more volume.

Whenever possible, let your hair dry naturally. My feeling is, the less wear and tear on the hair, the better.

Heated rollers are great for an emergency pickup for your hair. The Teflon-coated rollers are gentlest. But try to get a style that doesn't depend on them daily and don't leave them in your hair longer than five minutes. Constant use of any heating equipment can lead to dried-out hair.

Curling irons and hot combs can also dry out delicate hair. Be sure your hair is well conditioned and slightly damp before you use them. Remember, when you use any heat on your hair, you need to step up the conditioners.

How your head feels, and how your hair feels on your head, has a great deal to do with how you feel about yourself, how you think you look to yourself and to others. If you have a rigid hairdo, the chances are it will influence your feelings to some degree—you will feel rigid. You can't be totally free and relaxed with a stiff head of hair. One thing it is not is sexy.

There is a haircut, a hairstyle, a hair look that is right for you that looks natural and won't create problems that will consume your emotions and your time. The simpler the better, and the more elegant.

If you haven't made a change in years, you should try a new look for yourself, particularly if you have been constantly wounding your hair. You may not be as strong as you were in your youth, and neither is your hair. Risk a new style, but don't risk your hair.

More than anything, we need to work with ourselves to reveal the richness of our own natural beauty. Begin with that. Begin where you are now.

YOUR SKIN CARES

What commands attention,

demands responsibility—

Beauty.

HOW unique are you? Your skin holds the answer: There are no two people in all the world who have identical skin patterns. When you understand some of the things skin does besides covering you, you will want to give it the attention and respect it is due.

Skin is a living organ. It breathes. It helps control body temperature. It protects us from disease, from fluids passing through it into our bodies. It regulates oil production within our tissues. It talks to our brain, relaying messages of feelings, of sensations of pain or pleasure.

It is nearly beyond our comprehension in its beautiful and complex design and structure, and it is laid on the various parts of our bodies in different densities. It is thick in the areas that need thickness: the bottoms of the feet and the palms of the hands. In contrast, it is thin in the areas around the neck, upper chest, eyes, forehead and on the backs of the hands.

Every single cell in your whole body is alive. Each has its own special life. Collectively, the cells create structure. Skin is structured in three major layers: epidermis, dermis and subcutaneous fat layer.

The outermost layer, the epidermis, is covered by an acid mantle, just as your hair is. The cells of the epidermis have a life span of about two weeks before they slough off and are gone. But in an ongoing process of change and regeneration, new cells make their way from within to form this outer, protective layer of our skin.

The next layer is called the dermis. It is below the epidermis and is made up of collagen, an elastic protein fiber that binds surrounding tissues and itself to the epidermis to keep everything in place. The dermis plays a major role in regulating your body's temperature, acting like a thermostat, as well as in determining the texture of your skin. It also controls the amount of oil in your skin, which acts as a protective barrier to keep all but a minimal amount of outside fluid from being absorbed into your body.

Subcutaneous fat is the layer between the dermis and your internal organs. This layer supports nerves, sweat glands, and blood vessels and holds hair roots. It is like mobile insulation, giving your skin flexibility and cushioning.

You are mostly composed of fluid, and most of it is lymph. This fluid constantly circulates through the skin, an endless river of life. We are the original air-conditioners. Living ones. The lymph is very like sea water, though not identical. It carries necessary nutrients and minerals that nourish our living cells. This interior river must stay in constant motion circulating through the cells. If it doesn't, for any reason, the cells are deprived of essential "food" and die, which can bring illness or even death. In the natural world, circulation means life. If a stream or pond stagnates, it is declining or dying. We are not exempt from the same law.

We Are One with Creation

Our skin was made to be totally self-sustaining, self-regulating. It was made to police itself, carrying out its myriad functions. It is complete.

Healthy skin has elasticity and a moist quality, or, as the fashion magazines would say, a dewy look. It is problem-free. But skin has to breathe. It needs air to carry out its function of eliminating through the pores. It also needs stimulation, light, some sun, exercise and nutrition. Sound familiar? It's you.

Poor diet, too much sun, excessive cigarette smoking, too much alcohol, drugs, some say caffeine and alkaline soaps are all enemies of your skin. Anything that you do to yourself in a compulsive way may not be helpful in the long run. But if your skin is excessively dry or oily on its own and you are not contributing to that condition, it may be caused by an imbalance in your endocrine system and should be checked with a doctor. Today there is nothing available over the counter that cures an endocrine problem, though there is temporary help for the symptoms.

As our skin grows older and becomes thinner, it also loses elasticity, which shows up particularly in the areas that are already thin or fine: the lips, around the eyes, the forehead and the backs of our hands. On the neck and face, the skin crumples in on itself, helped by diminishing subcutaneous fat. Dehydration and loss of elasticity cause premature aging of the skin.

The sun is perhaps the main offender in contributing to loss of skin elasticity. For many people, this information comes too late. You cannot take back the past and all those hours spent unprotected in the sun. Those who practically worshipped the sun, as I did, unquestionably injured their skin to some degree.

The Sun—Your Not-So-Warm Friend

Sun-damaged skin is hidden from us for years. The damage is cumulative. If you had too much sun exposure in childhood, the damage is probably done by the time you are twenty years old, but it doesn't begin to show on the surface of your skin until you are in your forties or fifties. And the additional exposure in the years since your youth simply adds to the problem.

When you go into the sun, your skin cells work overtime in an extraordinary effort to produce the melanin needed to protect your hide. When the exposure is too great, they overproduce in a frantic effort to do their job. Eventually, this causes problems.

The thin skin areas on your body are the first affected and therefore the first to lose their elasticity and wrinkle. Wrinkling begins when the underlying structure of the skin is damaged by too much sun, when the dermis layer is injured and starts to break down.

Fair, freckled, blue-eyed and green-eyed people have the least amount of melanin and therefore the least resistance to the sun. They are a high risk for skin cancer. Everyone should stay out of the mid-day sun, but this rule applies particularly to light-eyed blondes and redheads.

Some sun is good for the skin, even important for it, but exposure should be built up slowly. Gradually. This allows the cells to keep pace in manufacturing enough protection.

When skin dries out from sun exposure and it shows, it is because the outer layer has not been able to retain enough protective oil and moisture. In fact, exposure to any kind of heat on a prolonged basis reduces the skin's natural moisture and oil content and is bad for it. The skin becomes parched and eventually brittle, just like leather. After all, leather is skin. The other extreme, cold, produces the same problems, evaporating the natural moisture and slowing down oil production.

Anyone on medication should check with a doctor before going into the sun because the sun's ultraviolet rays and radiation can produce an allergic reaction when certain medications are taken. Cosmetics and perfumes can also cause allergic reactions on sun-exposed skin because of the chemicals they contain. Unfortunately, some people are even allergic to sunscreens.

Sun creams and lotions contain varying strengths of protective ingredients to filter out damaging rays. The filtering ability of a product is called its sun protection factor, or SPF, and is rated on a scale from 2 to 23. The maximum protection—a complete and total blockout—would be an SPF of 15 to 23. You should have at least one total-blockout SPF 15 among your sun-care products. Use it on your nose, the V of your throat line and in those emergency situations when you're forced to be out in the sun too long.

Many sun products contain a member of the B complex vitamin family called PABA, para-aminobenzoic acid. You can also take PABA in pill form, which may help skin resist sunburn. Those people who are allergic to PABA should look for a hypoallergenic cream or lotion that is unscented and protective.

If your skin is very fair and you burn easily, it's best to begin with a high SPF of 10 to 12. Resign yourself to being a "fair lady," add color in your nail polish, use clearer, brighter lipstick and stock up on big sunhats. If you rarely burn and tan easily, begin with an SPF of 8 to 10 and step down to an SPF of 4 to 6 while deepening your tan. When you apply your sunscreen, don't forget these often neglected places: the neckline, right below the throat (golfers and tennis players often get too much sun here), the backs of the hands and the forearms.

Yes, tans look wonderful. They play up your hair color, they cover a multitude of skin sins, they make you look healthy. But a tan is not to be used as makeup! Get the healthy look with bronzers and blushers, not with more than a very light, sun-kissed look. Otherwise, you'll be sun-cursed by yellowing, faded color when the tan disappears, by loss of skin tone and texture and by premature aging and possible serious damage.

After any kind of sun exposure, it pays to use an after-sun lotion. Those with aloe vera gel are wonderfully soothing. Aloe vera has been used for centuries as a remedy for healing burns. Bad sunburns can be soothed almost miraculously by applying gel from the plant (which you can buy in health food stores) directly to the sore area.

In the last few years, significant strides have been made in providing the public with products that protect and moisturize. Some even claim they are able to increase the speed with which new cell growth occurs and thus help to repair damaged cell problems.

Invest a Little Extra Time in Your Skin

Science is paying attention to our skin problems. So should we. Your skin reflects the state of your health, which is a reflection of how you are treating yourself.

One of the ways to improve your skin's health and your overall health is to lay off sugar, starch, soda, caffeine, alcohol and junk food. Also, you should drink from six to eight glasses of pure water each day, since it is the best way to moisturize your whole system, including your skin. It is also the best way to keep your system—and your skin—properly flushed. Taking care of your complexion involves a little extra time each day. It is a small price, considering what your skin does for you and what you want from it—mere perfection.

Body skin and facial skin require slightly different considerations. Face skin is more fragile because of its thinner composition and because it is constantly exposed to the elements and to subtle erosion from polluted air. The backs of our hands are vulnerable, too.

No matter what type of skin you have—dry, oily, normal or combination— taking care of it involves these processes: thorough cleansing, freshening (restoring the protective mantle on the surface of the skin) and moisturizing.

The debate over cleansing with lotions, creams or soaps goes on. There is testimony from all sides, but as your skin demonstrates clearly, you are unique and your skin is specific in its needs. Finding the right cleanser is a case of trial and error.

If you do use soap, use an unscented one or one of the nonsoap cleansing bars. It should leave your skin soft and clear, not tight or irritated. It should loosen the layers of dead cells that accumulate and flush them away so the new cells can breathe. Be sure to rinse off your soap cleanser thoroughly, splashing your face with lots of warm water to hydrate the skin.

Next comes your freshener, applied with cotton balls to wipe away every last trace of soap. Some fresheners have an astringent added to tighten your pores, some are acidic to restore the acid balance on the surface of your skin. Some have healing agents, oils or menthol added.

After the freshener comes the all-important moisturizing cream. Moisturizers act as sealers to lock in the water you have just splashed on your face. They can also contain humectants, ingredients which attract moisture from the air, and lubricants, which protect the skin and add oils, proteins and other do-gooders. The sooner you apply them after you wash your face, the better job they do. Some even contain sunscreens, an excellent idea in summer.

Since the area around the eyes has no oil glands, you may need an eye cream with special lubricants for this area. And remember, any cream or lotion you apply to your face should be stroked on with an upward and outward motion. Never pull down. Keep everything up.

ESPECIALLY FOR DRY SKIN

Your skin, with its tiny, nearly invisible pores, can chap and easily become red and irritated from too much heat or too much cold. Cleanse with a very mild, superfatted creamy soap or a rich cleansing lotion or cream. If your skin becomes red, dry or flaky, you have the wrong soap for your skin. It should feel fresh and clean.

Choose a very light freshener with no alcohol.

Moisturizer is a must for you. Choose one especially formulated for dry skin. And since your skin is especially susceptible to sun damage, find one with a sunscreen added.

At night, put an extra-rich night cream on the driest areas. You should also consider using a humidifier in your bedroom to add moisture to the air and to your skin while you sleep.

Take a small bottle of moisturizer with you to reapply when your skin feels dry, especially in airplanes where the air is driest.

ESPECIALLY FOR OILY SKIN

Your skin has large pores that won't shrink, no matter what. Keep oils away from your skin. Cleanse with a nonoily cleansing bar or medicated soap. Follow with an astringent with a slight alcohol content. Keep a small bottle of freshener with you to cleanse oily spots during the day.

Use a very light moisturizer, with a minimum of oil, to protect your skin during the day. At night, you may only need a bit of moisturizer around the eye area.

Chances are, you have oily hair as well as skin. Wearing an off-the-face hairstyle and shampooing frequently can minimize blackheads on your forehead. Cutting out fried foods and cutting down on fat in your diet can help too.

ESPECIALLY FOR COMBINATION SKIN

You have small or medium pores, rather dry cheeks and an oily T zone (the forehead, nose and chin). Cleanse with a mild soap or cleanser and follow with a toner or freshener. Use a light moisturizer, day and evening, concentrating on the dry areas of your face.

Choosing the Right Products for Your Skin

Sorting through the mind-boggling array of skin preparations available today is a time-consuming task. You can save time (but not necessarily money) by going to the cosmetics department of your favorite store and buying all your products from one quality manufacturer. Most have a group of cleansers, moisturizers and toners geared for each skin type. The salespeople at the counter are usually very knowledgeable about the company's products and are trained to guide you. Or you can go the trial-and-error route of putting together your own group of products. Or you can go to a skin specialist and follow his or her recommendations.

If there is a good skin salon near you, its personnel can very accurately diagnose the condition of your skin after examining it under a special magnifying glass. They can tell you if your skin is dry from dehydration (lack of water) or from lack of oils. And they can suggest how to deal with this dry or dehydrated skin with moisturizers, emollients (which lubricate with oils and trap moisture in the skin) or humectants (which attract moisture from the air). The skin salon experts also do facials and remove blackheads and whiteheads—a task you should never attempt, no matter how tempting it is to squeeze them.

When you buy a product for your skin for the first time, buy the smallest size available or ask for a sample. You never really know what its true effect will be on your skin until you have used it for a while. If your skin is very sensitive, it will show irritation immediately.

SOAP AND WATER: THE BASICS

Soap is rarely just soap anymore. Most of the new products (or cleansing bars) are designed to do special things for your skin.

Natural soaps contain ingredients like honey, seaweed, lemon, aloe vera, chamomile and clay. These are very good for dry or sensitive skin because they often contain no extra chemicals (check the label, always).

Superfatted soaps are very gentle, great for dry skin. Dry skin can also benefit from soaps with cold cream, cocoa butter, coconut oil, olive oil and lanolin and soaps that contain milk or milk by-products.

Oily skin can be helped by a nonfatty soap, such as a transparent glycerin soap that adds moisture but not oil to the skin. It is highly soluble, rinses easily and disappears fairly rapidly. Other soaps to try: medicated, antibacterial soap to help blemishes; oatmeal soap that is mildly abrasive.

Most regular soaps that contain fragrance and deodorants should be confined to your body. They can make bathing a delight, but the fragrance is not recommended for facial skin.

When you wash your face, no matter what type of soap you choose, remember to rinse, rinse, rinse (splashing twenty to thirty times) to get the soap off and to hydrate your skin with water. And pat or blot your face gently, even leaving your skin slightly damp. Water is your skin's best friend. Apply your moisturizer to still damp skin. Give your face a spritz of mineral water from a perfume atomizer any time of the day.

Give your face a steam bath once or twice a month to open up and cleanse your pores (unless you have broken capillaries, in which case avoid extreme temperatures). Heat a quart of water in a large saucepan. You can add a tablespoon or two of herbs—chamomile, mint, comfrey or rosemary. When the water boils, take the saucepan to a low table. Make a tent of towels over your head and steam your face for five or ten minutes. It's a good idea to follow with a gentle, abrasive cleanser and a mask to tighten your pores and seal in the moisture.

If you have access to a steam bath, use that to give your whole body a steam treatment. I find saunas to be very drying to my skin. If you use a sauna, remember to drink lots of water and replenish your skin with moisturizers.

FACIAL MASKS

A good face mask once a week or so is another way of sealing moisture in your skin, drawing out impurities and tightening pores. The tightening power of masks that dry on your skin helps draw the blood to the surface, which is excellent for aiding circulation, the flushing, restoring process. Don't lose sight of the importance of that function, particularly as you get older and may not be as active as you were or should be.

You can buy all kinds of commercial masks for every skin type, or you can make your own from ingredients right in your refrigerator. Here are some ingredients you can use alone or in combination (I've found that equal portions of each ingredient works fine).

Mask ingredients for dry skin: Egg yolks, mashed bananas, peaches, avocados, olive oil, yogurt, powdered milk, cucumbers, sour cream, honey, brewer's yeast, lemon, grated carrots, cornstarch.

Mask ingredients for oily skin: Papaya, strawberries, tomatoes, lemon juice, oatmeal, cornmeal, brewer's yeast, cucumber, apple juice, whipped egg white and cornmeal or oatmeal, lemon juice, thyme.

Mask ingredients for normal skin: Chamomile, rose hips, strawberries, bananas, egg yolk, yogurt, mayonnaise.

Kitchen cosmetics are great fun. Mix your own recipes, then leave the concoction on your face (better, relax and lie down with your feet up) for twenty minutes. Rinse off with warm water. You'll be pleased with the difference in texture and the new glow of your skin.

EXFOLIATORS

Stimulation of the skin helps circulation. Exfoliating—which literally means removing scales or dead cells from the surface—not only stimulates circulation but helps the skin breathe by clearing away layers of useless cells and allowing it more freedom to absorb needed oxygen.

There are several ways to exfoliate your skin yourself, rather than having it done chemically. Use a rough washcloth, a coarse sponge, a complexion brush or a bigger, stiffer body brush. All can do the job of exfoliation. They stimulate your skin's natural action of knocking off the old cells and making room for new ones at the surface. The process of exfoliation is especially helpful to older skins because they don't shed cells as fast as they once did. Exfoliating, stimulating the skin any way you can that is safe and healthy, helps nature move a little faster and keeps your skin glowing. Be sure to apply a moisturizer to your face or a body moisturizer to your body after this treatment. Try to apply the moisturizing creams or lotions while your skin is damp, particularly if you have scrubbed—that is, exfoliated—yourself.

If you are considering any skin treatments more involved than that, consult a dermatologist, who can talk to you about chemical exfoliation or mechanical dermabrasion. The basic principles are the same as doing it yourself, but chemicals or machinery are involved.

On days when you are not busy scrubbing yourself in your bath or shower, it can be very nice and peaceful to take a warm bath and just relax. Soak for at least five minutes before adding oil or cream to the bath water. This gives your skin time to soften in the water, so that when you do add the oil, your skin is more receptive to it. When you get out of the bath, rub your body with your hands—a little body massage helps your skin absorb the oil. If you don't use anything in your bath except a good body soap, apply some oil or lotion when you get out.

Don't forget your feet. They may need extra attention, considering what they do all day, in addition to being imprisoned in shoes most of the time. If your feet have developed calluses and bumps from their years of imprisonment, use a pumice stone on them after you bathe, while the skin is still soft. It helps. Also be sure to massage them with whatever oil or lotion you use on the rest of your body. If they really need to be softened up, rub them with Vaseline, and wear a pair of socks to bed for the night.

The thin skin on the backs of your hands, like the skin on your face, is always exposed. It needs to be lubricated regularly, and I suggest more often than once or even twice a day. Keep hand lotion by your sinks, your bed, in your purse, wherever you are, so you can lubricate that skin at any time of day. Your hand skin not only is exposed, but is also constantly washed or submerged in water that is loaded with chemicals, etc. If you are outside a great deal, use a sunscreen on the backs of your hands as well as lotion. There are some sunscreen creams that provide both the protection and the moisturizing that your hands need.

If brown age spots have already appeared on the backs of your hands, there are bleaching creams available that can be purchased over the counter. Generally, these creams are controversial because they contain mercury, which should not be absorbed into your system. Some health food stores now carry ointments made from natural sources that are supposed to offer help in fading out the unwelcome brown spots. I do not know how successful these ointments are, but I do think if there was a sure cure we would all know about it. In the meantime, short of your dermatologist's suggestion and perhaps prescription, prevention is the best approach. Even if you already have brown spots on the backs of your hands, start using sunscreen to keep them from becoming worse.

And your lips. Dry, cracked lips are uncomfortable and aren't great-looking, either. Lipstick offers some protection, particularly if you buy the very creamy type or those that have protection built in. If dry lips are a year-round problem, you have to take added precautions. Use lip moisturizers, chapstick, Vaseline or Blistex. If none of these gives you relief, start counting the number of glasses of water you drink per day. Parched lips can be an indication of simple dehydration. Your lips can act as a barometer of the moisture in your system. Try not to lick your lips when they are dry in an attempt to make them feel better. It won't help and can aggravate the condition.

Try different products. Don't be afraid to make changes in what you use. Experiment just as you do with cosmetics. Rotate a few different products, alternating them. Our bodies need variety.

Over the years, a few inexpensive products have endured for decades because they are effective. Vaseline, lanolin, rubbing alcohol, witch hazel, castor oil, glycerin, baby oil, cold cream are examples of tried-and-true standbys for use on our skins.

Collagen in cream form can be helpful temporarily for dry skin and wrinkles. It binds moisture to itself and, while it stays on the surface of your skin, helps keep the cells moisturized and fattened up. But it treats only the symptoms, not the cause. Collagen injections into the skin are also thought to help fill in unwanted lines. Since their effects last only from six months to two years, they will always require redoing or supplementation. Some people are sensitive or allergic to outside collagen, which comes from cows.

Nature's Skin Helpers—Tried and True

Taking your skin savers directly from nature is nothing new. Many of these remedies are as good as any commercial preparations, and you run little risk of damaging or irritating your skin. You may recognize your grandmother's favorite remedy among the following:

Pore tighteners and fresheners: Lemon juice (diluted), apple cider vinegar (diluted), cucumber juice, ginseng tea, thyme brewed as tea.

Cleansing scrubs: Ground almonds or apricot kernels, oatmeal, cornmeal, cornstarch, seaweed.

Skin soothers: Chamomile, cucumber, aloe vera (good for healing sunburn), avocado. Milk in any form—whole, dry, skim, buttermilk, yogurt—can be added to a bath for sensitive and dry skin or used as a soother. Milk added to bath water is a good acid/alkaline balancer for the skin. Some say it lightens the skin a bit, too.

Deep cleanser: A mask of papaya or strawberries.

For puffy eyes: Cucumber slices, wet tea bags, potato slices, cotton pads saturated with chamomile tea or witch hazel.

To dry blemishes: Dot on lemon juice or garlic. Tomatoes and brewer's yeast are also thought to help blemished skin.

To stimulate circulation: Extract of ivy, which is now being used in many products aimed at controlling or breaking down cellulite.

To draw out and absorb skin impurities: Clay (kaolin) or mud packs.

A natural humectant: Honey or glycerin and rose water. Honey is good in a mask combined with egg whites or yolks.

Softening oils: Avocado, almond oil, primrose oil containing gamma linoleic acid, which is an essential fatty acid. These can be taken internally or used directly on the skin. Vegetable oils like safflower oil, wheat germ oil, coconut oil (or cocoa butter), peanut oil, sunflower oil and sesame oil are good. Animal oils like lanolin most resemble human oil. Jojoba oil was used by the American Indians on both skin and hair—a good moisturizer.

These ingredients are all natural and safe, unless you have an allergy to any one of them. Mix up your own beauty treatments. Experiment!

What to Eat for Your Skin

Vitamins A, D, E, B and zinc are all helpful to your skin, though you should consult a nutritionist to find out how much of each to take. Eating roughage to produce more efficient digestion will also help your skin bloom.

Diuretic cures can dehydrate your skin as well as your body. Avoid them if at all possible. Alcohol also dehydrates the skin.

Yo-yo dieting, when your weight goes up and down, can cause your skin to sag with every weight gain and loss. It can also worsen double chins and eye bags. Try to find your ideal weight and stick to it!

Respect your life

and you have beauty.

Plastic Surgery: Is It for You?

Skin grafting was used as a form of medical repair before the birth of Christ. It was again heard of in the fourteenth century in Italy. France furthered the work done in connection with skin grafting in the 1700s, as did other countries in Europe and, before long, the United States. Techniques were advanced in the last century until we have what today is referred to as cosmetic surgery.

Surgery to improve the shape of the nose has been the most popular throughout the centuries. While noses are still a matter of popular concern, so is sagging skin, particularly in the face and neck areas. Both sexes today are curious about what cosmetic surgery can do to repair or eliminate conditions they do not choose to live with for the rest of their lives. And why should they—or anyone?

If something bothers you and it can be fixed, fix it. We prune everything else in life to our personal satisfaction and tastes. I do not consider this desire anti-life or anti-anything. I do consider it a matter of personal aesthetics. And the point here is to have that concern for your look, your beauty, to have a sense of personal aesthetics.

Before any work is done, two things are essential for those who opt for cosmetic surgery. The first is the surgeon you choose. He or she must be excellent. Not adequate, excellent. He or she should be able to look at you with the eyes of an artist, to reconstruct like a sculptor, to understand your desires and thinking and tune in to your emotional state. The second point is that when you contemplate cosmetic surgery, particularly if it is a face-lift, understand that nothing is going to make you look as though you were in your youth again.

Cosmetic surgery is not a panacea for all face and body problems. It can smooth out skin, tighten it up and make you look better at any age, provided you really needed the help in the first place and were not just being paranoid about a line or two. I have known young models who live in terror of growing older. Not even old, just older. This phenomenon does not just apply to young female models, either. In fact, a model has more reason to undergo cosmetic surgery than most people, since she earns her living by her looks.

Cosmetic surgery does not necessarily remove lines. It does remove excess, sagging skin. Lines are smoothed out in this process but not removed. If all lines were removed from a face in mid-life, the person would look like they were made of plastic.

How much skin loosens and at what age varies with the individual. It is usually determined by inheritance, how much exposure you have had to the sun and elements, the state of your health, the type and condition of your skin as well as your facial bone structure. In some faces, the bone structure is so elegantly and advantageously formed that it keeps the skin taut for almost a lifetime.

Just as a face-lift is a matter of personal choice, so is the decision to have any of the other cosmetic surgical operations that are available today: eye lifts, removing the pouches and loose skin from underneath the eyes, reshaping noses, fixing ears that stick out, trimming jowls or droopy chin lines, not to mention body surgery such as breast reconstruction and resizing, stomach lifts, thigh tucks and buttock lifts.

HOW TO CHOOSE A PLASTIC SURGEON

With plastic surgery becoming more and more prevalent, clinics are springing up around the country. Some are little hospitals in themselves. Many offer lower prices than you would pay at a hospital. I would like to stress very strongly, however, that this is no time to bargain-hunt. Any kind of surgery can have complications. Although many people dismiss this surgery as easy and "cosmetic," it is still serious business. If your bargain-priced doctor botches your surgery, you'll have to either live with the results or spend far more money on reconstructive surgery to undo the damage.

Your best strategy is to get a doctor through the nearest university-affiliated teaching hospital or medical school. A physician affiliated with a school must have good credentials. You can also check the American Society of Plastic and Reconstructive Surgeons, Inc., at 233 North Michigan Avenue, Chicago, Illinois 60601 (tel. 312-856-1818), the professional association to which most plastic surgeons belong.

When you interview the doctor, and I suggest you see several (remember, this is your face), be sure to listen to what he or she thinks are the real prospects for success. Any unrealistic expectations you may have should be dispelled. You should also see some real-life examples of the surgeon's work, not just "before" and "after" photos. Finally, talk to people who have had the operation you are considering. Most patients are willing to help.

Many plastic surgeons have a specialty: eyes, noses, face-lifts, body surgery, breast reconstruction. Try to find out what type of surgery the doctor does most often. The more often he does the operation you want, the better.

I believe in helping yourself. Helping yourself to your own psychological peace and security. But it is important to remain realistic about what can be done and how you will look after the surgery. Demanding to be "nineteen" if you are forty-five or fifty is not realistic. Demanding to look like someone else is not, either. You should be the best you are able to be at whatever age you are. That can be terrific, and it is always something to strive for.

Other Possibilities

There are many other skin-reforming or -improving procedures that are beneficial when done skillfully by either a dermatologist or a cosmetic surgeon: dermabrasion and skin peeling to resurface your skin; cryotherapy to remove brown spots; electrodesiccation to remove broken capillaries; injections to heal acne cysts; the simple removal of whiteheads trapped beneath a cover of skin.

Blackheads that form in your pores, particularly if you have oily, large-pored skin, can be self-treated with thorough cleaning. Or you can go to a facial salon for periodic deep cleaning. Neither blackheads nor whiteheads should be squeezed, however.

There is a cream available over the counter that helps melasma, which is dark-colored spots that appear on the cheeks, temples and forehead. You do have to use it for a very long time to lighten the spots, though.

Body hair where you don't want it can be bleached, but if you choose to do this on your own, give yourself a patch test first. There is a mild facial cream bleach for upper lip hair. Electrolysis is a long, slow process, works best on small areas of the face and should definitely be done by a skilled professional. Waxing can be done at home with special kits found in drugstores. However, it is a very messy procedure and doesn't work for everyone. It can irritate sensitive skin and cause ingrown hairs. Better to leave it for small areas, such as the upper lip—or, better yet, have it done professionally.

What Your Hands Tell About You

Your hands and nails attract other people's attention. You can't hide them, and they tell an immediate story about you and your habits. If you use your hands constantly, it is almost impossible for them to look beautiful all the time. But you can keep them looking clean and in shape.

Anyone who has ever had a manicure can reproduce the process herself. The result may not be as good as the professional job, but it is fine for your everyday life.

Nails, like your hair, are dead and have no sensation. Just as hair is formed inside the hair follicle, your fingernails are formed inside your finger. So the way you treat your fingers affects the condition of your nails when they emerge from the cuticles. If your fingers have been injured or had a severe blow, your nails may well reflect the injury. Some authorities say that an overload of stress or strain will also affect the appearance of the nails.

To protect your hands, get in the habit of wearing gloves as often as possible: gloves in the cold, lined rubber gloves to wash dishes or to do household cleaning chores, gardening gloves, and thin white cotton gloves to wear to bed once in a while with your hands slathered in a rich cream (one famous hand model wears A and D ointment under her gloves overnight).

Cuticles that are in good shape, soft and healthy are important to the nails and their early growth. Massage a good cuticle cream into cuticles regularly to moisturize them. An occasional, even weekly, nail bath in warm lotion, Vaseline or vegetable oil will make a positive difference for your cuticles and will help the nails.

When the cuticle is lubricated and soft, take an orangewood stick, wrap the end with a little cotton and push the cuticle back. This is good for the cuticle and massages the nail bed—just as your hair and gums need massage, so do your nails. Don't force the cuticle: When you work with it, work gently.

After removing whatever lubrication you have used on your cuticles by brushing your nails in a little soap and warm water, shape the nails with an emery board or good nail file. Slant the file under the edges of the nails and then across the tops, always filing in one direction only.

Buffing your nails will give them a clean, smooth appearance. Always buff in one direction too, from the cuticle to the end of the nail. Use light, even strokes so friction won't build up on the nail. If your nail starts to get heated, stop. Try to find and use a chamois buffer.

If you dicide to use polish, which does add strength to your nails, use a base coat first, then one or two layers of polish, and finally a top coat. On older hands, a soft-color polish is better than a dazzling color or one with too much shine and glitter.

Weak nails that split and break can get some help from protein conditioners or strengtheners. Weakness can be caused by many things, including improper filing, overexposure to chemicals, vitamin deficiency, or excessive use of drying polish removers. Find a polish remover that is low in acetone and has a built-in conditioner. When your nail polish needs a touch-up, instead of removing the old polish, add a new coat on top. Try to use nail polish remover as little as you can. When you do use it, wash your nails immediately afterward.

Beautiful nails give you a beautiful, "polished" look. The gracefulness of your hands, their movements and appearance are all part of you and your beauty. Hands are not a foreign extension; they are a highly visible and personal statement about you that is very public.

TIPS FOR YOUR NAILS AND HANDS

- To help your polish last longer, don't forget to wear a top coat of clear enamel. Reapply a layer of top coat daily to keep the nails shiny and looking freshly polished. This also cuts down on chipping.
- To repair a crack or a break, use paper patches (available in nail repair kits), pieces of tea bag paper, a piece of a sheer Band-Aid.
- Be careful of nail extensions, sculpture nails and nail tips. These may be the only way many of us can have the look of long nails, but the application technique does damage the nail underneath and requires frequent and expensive "fill-ins." If you wish to try nail tips, it's best to have a professional apply them. And be very sure to keep them scrupulously clean, with an eye out for any signs of fungus developing under the nail.
- Use a strong sun block on the backs of your hands to keep any brown spots from deepening.
- The skin on the backs of the hands ages faster than other body skin because it has the least amount of subcutaneous tissue of any exposed part of the body except the eyelids—another reason for keeping your hands protected and under cover as much as possible.
- For brittle nails, try soaking them in warm olive oil before bedtime and leave a coating of oil on overnight.
- If your nails are slow to grow, it may help to buff them or massage the fingertips to improve circulation. Activities such as typing and piano playing are said to increase nail growth.

Treat Your Toenails Well

Toenails, while less public than fingernails, still require attention and care. The cuticles that guard your toenails are tough. They should be conditioned just like your fingernail cuticles, with a soak in good cuticle conditioner. Massaging with Vaseline or oil can help soften them, too.

Use the orangewood stick with cotton to push back the toenail cuticles. Instead of a nail file, use toenail clippers and clip straight across the tops of the nails. File the edges a little to soften any sharpness left from clipping. File in one direction only.

As a form of routine maintenance to keep the skin on your feet as well as the nail cuticle soft, massage your feet every day (better, twice a day) with a foot or body lotion, before encasing them in their leather prisons. At night, in place of lotion, try Vaseline and wear light cotton socks to bed. This prevents tough skin buildup and softens calluses and corns that are already there.

Soaking your feet in warm water makes them feel better. Epsom salts added to the soaking water is also therapeutic. A fast rinse with very cold water is a nice stimulating touch, good for skin circulation, too.

For hand and foot maintenance, you should have a good lotion for the hands and feet readily available. Nail scissors, toenail clippers, orangewood stick, fine-grain emery boards, a natural-bristle nail brush are your very basic pieces of equipment. Then you can add cuticle clippers to pare hangnails, a nail buffer to give natural sheen and polish and stimulate the nail beds, and buffing powder.

FOOT CARE TIPS

- The sole of the foot is said to contain nerve endings that connect with every part of the body. Learn to give a good foot massage to soothe your feet (and those of someone you love).
- There are lots of good foot-smoothing tools for removing calluses and rough skin. Invest in a good pumice stone or an abrasive "foot file" with a long handle and a sandpaperlike surface. Great for hard-to-reach areas.
- Pamper your feet by adding your favorite bath oil to the foot-soak water.
- Go wild and wear bright, vivid toenail polish. It's your reward for taking good care of your feet.

Preventive Measures: The Best Help There Is for Skin

Science is learning more all the time about the functions of our skin and how to help it repair and sustain itself by moisturizing, nourishing and stimulating its natural processes. But because one of the skin's many functions is to protect us from outside materials or invaders, only minute amounts of even sympathetic product ingredients will be "taken in" by it. So preventive measures are still the best help there is for skin, though I do think product help is important, too. Here are some preventive measures you can take:

- Moisturize from within: Drink six to eight glasses of water a day.
- Eat skin-loving foods. Cut out junk food, stimulants and chemicals that are hard on body and skin.

- Massage your skin to stimulate fluid circulation.
- Take baths and showers in medium warm water. Sustained heat or cold dehydrates or dries out skin, removing natural lubricants and protective oils.
- Manicure nails regularly for their health as well as their appearance.

No woman wishes to have deep lines etched into her face. But in truth, few are as unsightly as we are made to feel they are. Why has no one told men that the lines nature brings to their faces in mid-life are unacceptable? On the contrary, in men we accept them. We were never conditioned against them. The mid-life woman is the *only* person of either sex who is held up to comparison in terms of beauty. The young female is not, the very old female is not, men are not at any age, but the mid-life woman is.

I don't object to the helpful products, but I do object to the "attitude" that is used to sell them to us. It is a negative and scary approach. I don't like the insinuation that I have to look as though I were in my youth forever, that if I have lines in my face I won't be considered beautiful or sexually acceptable.

Advertising has relentlessly stimulated our fears. Deeper fears than the lines in our faces. The fear-nerve it hits is that life is somehow slipping away, getting by us, and the lines somehow represent this slippage of time. Yes, we all want to hold on to life, but no potion or lotion will give us extra years of living. What should be understood is that we want to look wonderful as we move along, not that we *have* to look young to gain acceptance. One of the fastest ways I know to lose years is to waste time fearing that your look or image is not sufficient for or acceptable to society.

The word "life"—the fact of life—is itself positive. Women in mid-life must begin to enjoy and be proud of their looks and recognize their beauty in every dimension, including the physical. What should be changed is not the natural lines in our faces but our perceptions of ourselves. We should pay attention to where our self-absorption is focused. We need to learn to agree with ourselves that we are beautiful, and stop agreeing with outside forces that suggest otherwise.

Yes, it would help if advertising told us we were beautiful, but if it doesn't, don't wait for it. You can tell yourself.

YOU DRESSING YOU

Use the power of thought

to create beauty. You.

AGE? Clothes? What do age and clothes have to do with each other? Very, very little.

You select the particular clothes you buy for many reasons. A "look" you want, a style, a color, a shape, a silhouette, a whim, a desire or even a fantasy, and sometimes just plain earthy practical need. Okay. But never, ever go shopping to look for clothes for your age. Don't do that to yourself.

There is no such thing as clothes for a forty-year-old or a fifty-year-old or a sixty-year-old. There are only clothes that are right for you or wrong for you. Clothes that work for you or don't work. Clothes that are right for you give something to you. Literally. They add positively to your appearance. They automatically look tasteful and appropriate. Not appropriate for your age—appropriate *for you.*

A woman who has lost her figure may well have to shop to create a different "look" than she used to have. This is not a matter of age but a matter of shape. Obviously if you have kept your figure, your choices are greater. Clothes look better on someone of any age who is in shape because that person looks better.

Once again, how we choose to dress has to do with our attitude about ourselves. We're back to self-image again. It's a matter of how you perceive yourself with your inner eye and senses. Your dress will make more of a positive or negative statement about your self-image than almost anything else.

How much society influences the way we dress may depend on the indi-

115

vidual. For most of us, the influence is tremendous. Over the last twenty-five years—the years of youth madness—advertising and fashion have established the idea that there is a connection between age and dressing. We have been saturated with the pervasive attitude that, apparently, only young people wear clothes. Older women don't. Or, if they do, who would want to see them?

Until the past few years, almost all fashion advertising and modeling was done by young girls. Today there are some token visual offerings for the older woman. I am occasionally used in them. But when fashion photos do use an older model to show the mid-life woman, the magazines often treat that woman with "special consideration," rather than just showing her as beautiful and viable, as central to our society as a young girl. In other words, it's as if the older woman, in fashion terms, has some special disease.

Not Being Twenty Is the Disease

Few women's magazines ever use the mid-life model to appeal to the mid-life woman editorially. This makes it extremely difficult to demonstrate the truth of how much chic, style and beauty a woman can have at this age. When you consider that probably 90 percent of the society photographs you see in a fashion paper like *W* show women well into mid-life as the crème de la crème, it becomes ironic that every fashion photo and ad shows clothes on the young and only the young.

The fashion industry lives in a world of pretend. In advertising terms, it pretends there are no women in the country over thirty or thirty-five. But the facts are different. As I mentioned earlier, the mid-life woman is the major clothes buyer today and she spends the most money. Her dollar has four times the buying power of that of the young, and that amount is increasing every year. All the statistics indicate this trend. And still . . . and still . . .

Indeed, why should fashion and advertising change? They make billions of dollars doing it the way they do. Why? Because they have a captive audience in every woman from thirty up. They know you will buy anyway. And you do.

The result is that mid-life women are forced to contemplate all fashion on the "nineteen"-year-old body. You, the money-spending public, are left to translate the picture into your own self-image. And the question all older women ask is: Are the clothes on that young model all right for me to wear?

Confusion. Intimidation. Yes? No? You don't know.

Millions of women feel confused, unsure and left out. Millions more take those pictures literally. They accept the picture at face value and deduce that the clothes on the model are meant to be worn by a young woman. Usually this is not true. Most mid-life women who have stayed in shape can wear probably 90 percent of the clothes shown in fashion pictures.

The fact that there is now at least token representation of the mid-life woman in fashion advertising is a step in the right direction, but that representation *should* be more than token. *In the meantime, we have to learn to know ourselves and how to be secure in the clothes we choose to wear.*

Your Body, Not Your Age, Determines What You Can Wear

Body structure alone determines the style and type of clothing you can wear successfully. Each one of us is a living clothes hanger for what we wear and "show" in public. You should give your body all its possible advantages in the way you dress.

No one has to look frumpy at any age. Ever. Young or old. What makes someone look frumpy? Sometimes it happens when women dress for a specific age rather than for themselves. Thinking they have to dress a certain way because they are a certain age, they look for a dress that says age. But usually it is a combination of things: poor posture and body movement, poor proportions in the clothes, drab colors, bad fit, cheap fabrics, wrong style or no style. All of this can be compounded by the wrong hairstyle for your face and body shape. Obviously, cleanliness and grooming count, too.

If your attitude is open, positive, alert and alive, you can avoid frumpiness with caring observation and by being willing to experiment and see yourself in new ways. You have to learn to know what makes you look good. It does not matter whether you are wearing jeans or an evening dress, you can always look good. How about beautiful?

There are a few articles of dress that are best left to the young in body: very tight shirts or blouses, see-through dresses or blouses, supertight pants or jeans and mini (I don't mean short) dresses and skirts. These are the only concessions I make to age in my dressing. Gimmick dressing is for kids.

But dressing is not about fads, gimmicks and designer labels. No designer label in tbe world can make something look right on you if it doesn't suit your body. Proportions, fabric, color, style, fit and accessories are what you need to dress yourself to your best advantage. These are the basics. The most important image or thought you can hold in your mind as you deal with the basics and select your clothing is simplicity. Simplicity of style.

There are just so many ways a jacket, dress, pair of pants, shirt or skirt can be cut, and there really are very few. Learn to look for clothes simple in design and appearance. Classic styles. Simple. Elegant.

You can be "with it" and still keep your own special, appropriate style. It's a matter of attitude. Women in mid-life and older were brought up with a much more rigid attitude toward clothing than what prevails today. Prim, stiff looks have given way to more fluid clothes that are easy to move in. These new clothes don't just belong to the young, in spite of what we see in photographs and on the runways. Today's styles are for every age. You *do not* have to dress in a way that says, "I am supposed to dress like this because I am no longer young."

Elements That Prevail at Any Age

It is much better to have a few quality items than a closet full of junk clothes. Good fabrics feel good and make you feel good wearing them. Cheap fabrics and bad synthetics can work against you. They are often stiff and shiny. They may be uncomfortable and fall apart easily. Many of the non-porous fabrics are hot and sticky; they don't allow your skin to breathe. Cheap, synthetic materials will never be elegant. They lack essence and inherent value. Learn to read labels so you know exactly what kind of fabric you are buying and remember to check inside linings as well.

FIT

A good fit is absolutely essential to looking good in clothes at any age. Don't try to cheat on the fit and pretend it's okay when it really isn't. And don't believe the salesperson who tells you it looks terrific. It may look all right but not feel right, and only you will know.

Be picky. When you try on something new, check yourself in a three-way mirror to see if the garment pulls anywhere—across your bust, your stomach, your thighs, your behind. See if there are wrinkles in the material in strange places where they don't belong, like across your shoulders or in the crotch area. Is the sleeve, jacket, skirt or pants length correct? Can you sit comfortably? Walk comfortably? Move your arms comfortably? Eat comfortably? If you are not completely comfortable, you will not feel right and you will end up not wearing the piece more than once or twice, no matter how much it cost.

Check the stitching both inside and out, as well as buttons and zippers. Are they in the right place on you, or are they hitting you in a place that won't ever look right? It's your money—make sure that you're paying for a good fit.

COLOR

Be sensitive to what the color of your clothes does to you. Does a particular color complement your skin? Hair? Eyes? Does it make you appear inviting, appetizing?

I think there are very few absolutes about color. Yes, there are some that will definitely be unbecoming on you. You will know them almost instantly. Instead of giving you a warm vibrant look, they steal from your natural coloring and leave you looking drained, yellow or pea green. Uninviting.

You are unique and should select your colors accordingly, but there are some generalities. Dark colors can make you look smaller. Light colors enlarge. Darker complexions can wear bright, intense colors better than fair skins, which look better in paler shades. Dark gray hair can wear bright colors, but pale gray hair looks better in soft colors.

Experiment with color. You will learn which colors make your eyes brighter, your skin tones warmer, your figure slender. When you try on something new in a store, don't trust the artificial lighting. Take the garment to a window so you can see its color in natural light. That is the only way you can be sure that you are getting the color you think you are buying.

STYLE

While checking yourself in a three-way mirror, check your silhouette, the overall shape you and the clothing make together. You should be enhanced by the shape of the garment you are wearing. If you want to hide or camouflage some areas of your body, look for a shape or style to achieve that for you. Also use clothes to create for you. For instance, wide shoulders make hips look narrower. A full blouse or bodice can give you a fuller-looking bust. Pleats in trousers and skirts disguise a too full stomach. A just-right belt can give you a smaller-looking waistline.

Become conscious of what kinds of clothes serve you well. For any specific style, there are many small adjustments you can make to help it work for you: pushing up sleeves, turning up a collar, not wearing a belt or wearing

119

one on your hips instead of at your waist, adjusting the length to cover or reveal. Details count. Become style-conscious for yourself.

The most expensive fabric, used to make the most perfectly tailored article of clothing, may still look unsuitable, awkward, even frumpy, if the proportions of the clothes are wrong for your body and build. As little as a quarter of an inch can make a difference in achieving the right look. The elegant, classy look. Lengths are critical—lengths of skirts and dresses, lengths of jackets worn with pants, lengths of pants, lengths of sleeves. If they are wrong by even a small amount, they can throw off the good look you want.

Shapes of clothing have a lot to do with the proportions, too. For instance, your jacket—whether it's short and fitted or long and loose—must work with the length and shape of your skirt, with the shape of your body as a whole and with the fabric. Every article of clothing seems to have its own personality, so keep an eagle eye alert for the proportion and the design it creates.

FABRIC

The elegantly simple classic styles you look for are best when constructed from fabrics that work—that last, that breathe, that do what they are meant to do. These most successful fabrics are usually the beautiful, natural fabrics like wool, silk, cotton, linen, velvet, corduroy, gabardine. They have been tried and tested forever. There is nothing unknown about how they work in clothing, and they won't become suddenly obsolete.

Yes, it means they will cost more, and "more" is plenty today. I know. I don't get free clothing because I am a model. I pay for everything I buy, just as you do. But cheap fabrics can, in effect, steal from you because they make you feel the way they are—not quite worthwhile.

Different fabrics can be used together beautifully. Different textures playing off and with one another can create a wonderful sense of luxury and great good looks. With a little imagination and flair, you can make a rich statement about yourself.

Accessories: Small Additions That Make a Big Difference

Accessories make magic. They are the touches that help snap an outfit into shape, give it spark, make it come to life. Unconscious to conscious. Accessories can make the difference between being noticed and not being noticed in the best possible way: affirmatively.

A touch of added color. A small splash somewhere. A belt or sash that makes an interesting addition. A small silk or cotton scarf sticking out of a pocket or tied at your neck. A large wool or silk textured or patterned scarf arranged around your neck and throat or just loosely thrown around your shoulders. Good-looking, simple elegant shoes, whether heels or flats. The one or two pieces of jewelry that make everything look sharp, including you. (Jewelry doesn't have to be real. Good fake jewelry can be handsomely ornamental.) Even the buttons on your coats or jackets can say a lot.

Accessories are points of attraction. They are spots to which the eyes gravitate. With the help of an accessory, you can play up your best features. Earrings with or without color will affect your eyes. Smart-looking cuffs and good-looking jewelry at your wrists show off beautiful hands. A belt with an unusual buckle will show off your waist or hips.

Stockings with fancy patterns and bold colors are okay for fun and games, but that's about it. They are often too costumey for serious dressing. Ornate patterns (though often very beautiful) take over all of you—your legs may be incredible, but you do want people to notice the rest of you, too. Patterned stockings with simple, stylish clothes steal from the clothes. They are not slimming to the leg, and few can wear them really successfully. Stockings need to work with the clothes you are wearing. Keep them in tones that help achieve long lines. If you want your legs to look just like "legs," keep a stash of nude, seamless stockings on hand.

Eyeglasses should be treated as an accessory as well as a cosmetic. And they are so terrific-looking today, one would hardly realize they are essential life equipment. The correct shape and proportion for your face, along with a flattering-colored frame or tint in the lens, can create a sexy, interesting, intellectual, sporty or sweet look. Depends on what you want. Different looks for different times or occasions. Then there are always contact lenses. I use both glasses and contacts. Recently I splurged and bought a second pair of contacts that are light aquamarine. I bought them for fun and they are fun! Intensely bright-eyed from time to time, I think my eyes might actually glow in the dark.

SHOES THAT GIVE YOU LONG, BEAUTIFUL LEGS

- The perfectly plain shell pump. When paired with hosiery of the same color, you can't beat the shell pump for giving you a long, unbroken leg line. V throat and low-cut insteps will add to the long-leg effect. These are also the best shoes if you have very large feet because they don't call attention to themselves.

- Shoes whose color blends with your hose. This is an old Hollywood trick for achieving the longest-looking legs. Wear taupe, beige or flesh-colored shoes that match your stockings. Also great in black with sheer black stockings.
- Open toes or designs at the toe of the shoe. This draws the eye down and away from the leg—one reason why the classic Chanel pump is so flattering.
- Sling backs. These make the expanse of the leg go right down to the heel.
- Toe cleavage. Very low-cut throats of the shoes, which show part of the toes, make the foot and the leg look longer.

Some Common Mistakes

As I travel around the country, I see these mistakes frequently—and they are so easy to correct!

Exposing too heavy upper arms. Unless your biceps are as slender and toned as a sylph's, keep them under cover. Short sleeves that cut the upper arm in two and sleeveless dresses are no-nos. Keep your sleeves down to the elbow (or roll up long sleeves) at least.

Wearing tight-fitting clothes to look thinner. It has just the opposite effect. You look like a sausage. Wear something a little larger instead, for a slenderizing effect.

Wearing clinging fabrics. Wear soft materials that drape and hang beautifully but don't cling.

Wearing very heavy fabrics from the waist down. Unless you are a beanpole, this will add pounds to your appearance.

Too much bulk at the neck. This can make you look "stuffed," unless you have a swan neck. Also pay attention to the right color at your neckline and how if affects your skin tone.

Wearing a tight belt at the waist accentuates a protruding stomach.

"Naked" elasticized waists. Wear a pretty belt or sash to finish the look. Or wear a shirt or blouse over the waistline.

Overdone jewelry. This can detract so much from you. If you have a strong dramatic piece, let it make a statement alone. Don't pile on gold chains, gold rings, gold earrings—and I still see charm bracelets. You may have a few beloved pieces, but not all of them all the time.

Stripes that overwhelm. Used well, vertical stripes can elongate you, horizontal stripes widen you. Be sure you want the effect they create.

Last year's flash fads. Maybe you can indulge in one or two, but throw them away when their time runs out. While you're wearing them, put them to use with your basic classic styles, a little as if you were tastefully mixing antique and modern furniture.

Dominating patterns. Solid colors are usually more flattering than patterns, unless the pattern is very small or you are very slim.

The wrong colors for your coloring. Soft, muted colors work very well and are almost always flattering on older women. Dark tones are the most slimming, but often are not flattering to the face (wear another, flattering color close to the face). Light, bright colors are enlarging (light expands)—see which ones add a lift, which ones overwhelm you.

Unrelieved black. Black can be tough to wear against an older, thinner skin, unless you have dramatic, strong coloring and the verve to carry it off. Fair, delicate, light-skinned women need to watch that it doesn't drain them of color. I wear it close to my face only if it is broken with a white collar, or if I can use a color or print scarf, pearls, something.

Beauty can be a matter of

---

condition and not years.

Unlike age, we *create* our

---

condition.

Clothes That Travel Well

When you travel, you need to get the most mileage from the fewest clothes. That's why it's so important to have separates that mix and match and a versatile, uncomplicated scheme of two or three colors at the most (perhaps two neutrals and one accent color). You can then mix different textures and patterns for variety, but try to stay within the same color family as much as possible.

123

I've found that *pale neutral colors* travel best to the most places and have a no-season chic. Off-white (oatmeal, wheat, linen white), pale gray, beige, camel and tan mix together beautifully and look as good in Texas as they do in New York. Elegant dark shades work best in Northern cities and in Europe, but may be too somber for Los Angeles or Atlanta. Save the bright colors for blouses or accessories.

While you're on the road, wear loose, comfortable clothes (but not too casual or sloppy). Avoid anything that binds or bunches up. Take a coverup that can be stowed away easily, pulled out for sudden changes of climate or blasts of air-conditioning.

A small travel steamer is the best way to remove wrinkles quickly and easily. You can find one in most appliance stores for under twenty dollars. Steamers are far easier to use than travel irons and are very kind to delicate, silky fabrics. You can also leave your clothes on hangers while you steam them, eliminating the search for an ironing board.

The key to no-fuss traveling is coordination in advance. Accessorize each outfit fully and try it on for a "rehearsal" before you pack. You can save valuable time hunting through your suitcase for the right accessories if you keep special hosiery or jewelry in little plastic sandwich bags, one for each outfit.

Finally, always take along a swimsuit and an exercise outfit. There is nothing that helps jet lag more than a long walk, a workout or a swim when you arrive.

On the Job—You're Selling Yourself!

The visual impression you make on the job can be crucial to your career, particularly if your job involves meeting the public. People focus first on what they see, and they should see you at your best—cool and in control.

What kind of office clothes you wear depends on where you work. Some offices have unwritten dress codes, while others are very casual. But casual never means sloppy, sexy or inefficient-looking. Anything that detracts from your work, like too much jewelry, garish colors, or inappropriate styling, is sure to hold you back.

On the other hand, there is no need to get carried away by the dress-for-success philosophy. You can put together a simple, classic work wardrobe that doesn't look like a second-rate version of what men wear. There is room for personality and flair, for beautiful tailoring and fabrics, for perfect fit, for touches of dash.

One thing to consider is whether or not you have to project authority. Are you a "boss" in charge of many people? If so, a coordinated look with suits or related separates will give you more presence. You should never look sloppily put together. Colors that blend, jackets or vests, a more tailored look, crisp blouses will help you look in control, well organized. *When you're in charge, quality details count.* Put your money into tasteful accessories: beautiful real jewelry in very elegant shapes, a lovely wristwatch, a luxurious leather handbag or briefcase, the perfect shoes.

If you see the same people every day, you will need more mix-and-match separates to give you a variety of office looks. Buying a series of separates from the same manufacturer will often give you maximum versatility because these clothes were designed to work together. A collection of beautiful blouses is another wardrobe stretcher.

Finally, is your job sedentary, or do you move around to many different locations? If you are on your feet all day, you need clothes that move well and don't bind. Your skirts should have enough ease in the fit to accommodate movement. Your clothes should stand up to wear and tear and, above all, be comfortable. Such clothes aren't always easy to find, so when you do find something that works well for you, consider buying it in several colors. It could make your life a good deal easier.

You will also have to pay careful attention to your shoes. Don't cut corners here—sore feet can make you irritable and you don't need that. Try buying several pairs in the same color (related to your hosiery) but with different heel heights so they can be switched around during the day.

When You're in the Spotlight

When you have to speak before a group or appear on television, you want people to pay attention to what you say, not what you wear.

On stage or before a group, think of your overall head-to-toe proportions. Aim for a slim, graceful line with very few distracting details. Stay away from clothing that cuts you in the middle and, if you wear a jacket, be sure it is well proportioned for your figure. Be sure to wear a skirt with enough fullness to sit and move well. Practice sitting with your knees together, angled slightly to the side, with one leg a bit in front of the other for the most graceful seated posture on stage. Crossed legs are usually deadly: Your calves look heavier and your skirt rides up.

To command attention you can wear a bright color—like red or cobalt blue—if there is one color that is especially becoming to you. But it's usually better to wear medium-toned, more elegant neutrals. That way, your clothes don't steal attention from you.

On television, soft neutral colors are also the most becoming. You should wear a pale color near your face to create a flattering light. (Choose soft ivory rather than stark white, however.) Keep the lines above your waist very simple and pay extra attention to your jewelry. No dangling earrings! Small, tasteful, tailored shapes with minimum glitter are best. You don't want earrings to distract from your face, but you may need them to add interest and a finished look. If you wear glasses, wear very simple pastel frames with clear lenses.

High necklines with no jewelry are usually best if your neck is wrinkled. If you wear a bow or scarf at your neckline, be sure it is beautifully tied and blends with your blouse. This is not the time for obvious accessories at the neckline.

Finding Your Own Fashion Expert

I believe it's best to be your own fashion expert. But some of us, no matter what we do, never look pulled together. Perhaps you are too close to yourself to be objective. Or perhaps you simply do not have the fashion sense, the time to shop or the knowledge of what's available in your city. If your appearance doesn't quite make it, get help from an objective, savvy source.

You can find your own fashion consultant. Depending on where you live, this could be a professional stylist who comes to your house and "weeds" out your closet, editing your wardrobe and mercilessly tossing out those mistakes you've worn only once. She'll then supplement what does work with new purchases.

She could be a professional shopper who shops the city for you (and other clients) every season and actually plans your wardrobe from scratch. You're paying for her expertise in fit and suitability and for editing the city's resources for you. No more buying a turquoise jacket that goes with nothing in your closet! Professional shoppers often know manufacturers who let them buy directly from the showroom at wholesale prices, saving you considerable money. Most shoppers charge for their shopping time and for a consultation and may also get a percentage from the store on what they sell to you. However, a professional really takes the hassle out of shopping and can be a lifesaver for the busy working woman.

Another option is the personal shopping service of a large department store. These shoppers comb the store to find just what you want and gather it all in one special dressing room. You then come in and try everything on at your leisure. There's no obligation to buy. Another fashion guru could be someone at a small boutique who has exquisite taste and always comes up with an outfit perfectly suited to your needs.

Many women rely on the taste of a friend or family member. I don't really recommend this. These people are used to seeing you a certain way and may have you "frozen" in a fashion mold. They also won't have the professional eye that can pick just the right pants shape for your figure, the perfect accessory to update your suit, or a new length for your hemline.

Expert help does not come cheaply, but neither do wardrobe mistakes with the price of clothing these days. A fashion pro can also give you an extra boost of confidence. You'll know you look your best. You'll also see yourself in a new way, wearing clothes that are in style, that you may have never considered before. What an interior designer does for a room, a fashion consultant can do for you. That's something to think about.

Dressing Well: It Takes Practice

One psychological study reveals that people form an opinion of you in the first fifty seconds of meeting. Yet another says twenty seconds. Obviously, that opinion is based on your appearance.

From childhood on, women want to make a statement of beauty both for themselves and for others. And they can. But it takes practice, particularly in selecting clothes. Knowing what to look for. It means trying on, eliminating, reorganizing, rethinking options about what you might have in your wardrobe. It could mean making room for previously untried looks. Mistakes? Of course. But just keep on trying, caring, observing, and after a while you will know what is right.

I frequently change my clothes two, three or even four times before I get my outfit "right" for the day or evening. I know when something "feels" wrong. I want a feeling of right, and what is right one day can be wrong the next. One day I may want a long skirt, the next a short skirt. It has a lot to do with where I have to go and what I have to do. I just keep trying until my instincts ring true—I've got it! But I am always working with clothes I like individually.

When you do feel right in your clothes and know you look the way you want to, then all is right with the world. Your world. That's a good start for a day or evening.

A Look Inside My Closet: Clothes for All Seasons

Certain kinds of clothes, other than the obvious ones like bathrobe and slippers, lingerie, stockings and shoes, know no season. They are year-round dressing staples. I keep the following seasonless clothes available in my closet or bureau all the time.

JUMPSUITS

It's useful to have a couple of tailored, medium-weight cotton jumpsuits in different colors. They can be worn very casually or can be dressed up with heels and jewelry. In the winter I can wear a turtleneck sweater or jersey underneath or a jacket on top. I change belts or use a sash. You can do a lot or a little. You can wear them with sneakers and forget everything else. When you are in a jumpsuit, you are dressed. They are convenient, they are easy and they work if they fit right.

TEE SHIRTS

I have tee shirts with long sleeves, short sleeves and just straps like old-fashioned undershirts. I have some with round necks, boat necks, mandarin collars, scooped necks. My favorites are men's oversized, all-cotton tee shirts that come three in a pack for very little money and can be found at your local five-and-dime store. They shrink a lot in the washer and dryer and end up still being too large, but are the right size for the way I wear them. Loose and easy.

I wear them with jeans. I wear them under wool sweaters that feel itchy in the winter. They also add a layer of warmth, which men have known for years. I wear them in the summer with cotton skirts, cotton slacks and shorts. I even wear them sometimes for casual dress-up with jewelry or with a scarf or sash at my waist. I wear them under loose-fitting, unstructured jackets, even structured jackets.

When they reach the point where I think they are no longer elegant enough for public wearing, they turn into nightgowns. They accomplish everything I want. They keep my shoulders covered at night and don't get caught up and twisted around me while I sleep. I do have a couple of real nightgowns, pretty ones. But I honestly prefer my tee shirts, as unglamorous as they are. They are comfortable. I keep the pretty nightgowns for special occasions. Really special. Otherwise, it's love me, love my tee shirts.

EXERCISE CLOTHES

Exercise clothes used to be known as "sweat clothes." They have come into their own. Today, they are good-looking, comfortable, useful, practical. Just very nice to wear.

I have sweat pants and shirts in white and navy blue. They are interchangeable. I believe women of any size can wear these colors. Matching tops and bottoms can even make you look slimmer.

I jog or walk in them in the city. I wear them around the apartment. I wear them in the country, and if I lived in the suburbs, I would wear them throughout most of any day while doing errands, shopping or just being at home and comfortable. I might even wear them to exercise in. They are a welcome addition to anyone's closet.

I would much rather see older women of any size in these clothes than in those god-awful housecoats that have been around for years, have zero style and are aging and demoralizing in a big way. I have modeled them. The minute I put them on, I feel as if I've turned into a frump. An old one. Most of them are totally sexless, too, and that won't do.

SHIRTS

White cotton long-sleeved shirts. Tailored for women and tailored like a man's for women. Men's-style shirts in pink, blue and stripes, too. Polo shirts, cotton turtleneck shirts, silk shirts (man-tailored and a little large) and white cotton shirts with ruffles at the cuffs and edging the collar. Shirts with no collars. Denim shirts, short-sleeved cotton shirts. These are used year-round with skirts, pants, shorts and sometimes under a jumper or tunic top. They can be worn informally or be dressed up with pearls or gold or silver jewelry— even diamonds. Almost any combination can be layered for wear during cooler weather. I frequently wear a cotton turtleneck under a long-sleeved shirt with a jacket over it all.

SWEATERS

There aren't enough sweaters in the world to make me happy. I love them. Sweaters in basic colors—beiges, tans, grays, navy, white and black—are the "glue" for any wardrobe unless you live in a hot climate. The addition of a few pastel-colored sweaters is useful and pretty. Most of the sweaters I have (accumulated over years) are regular length. Plain, old-fashioned, classic sweaters in wool, cashmere or cotton. I do have a couple of short-length sweaters that are easy to tuck into pants or skirts. Also a couple of long, loose, bulky-knit sweaters for casual wear, or to be worn with a silk shirt underneath and over a pair of good-looking, well-cut pants in gray or black to give me a dressy look. These same sweaters are very successful worn with soft, shin-length cotton skirts in warm weather.

Any sweater can be dressed up or down. They can be worn both over and under shirts. Add a small print scarf at your neck or an ascot-type silk scarf and you have yet another look.

Expensive sweaters with knit-in designs can be terrific-looking and fun to have. They are more expensive and, while they offer a different sweater look, they are not as versatile as solid-colored sweaters. If you can afford one for your collection, great!

EVENING CLOTHES

A soft, white, slim-legged pair of silk pants and two tops, one in a beautiful gray, another in a deep rose, give me instant, serious evening clothes for most occasions.

The silk tops are loose, boat-necked, with wide flowing sleeves and are long enough to softly cover my derriere. I wear them with silver or gold evening sandals and handsome gold or silver accessories, or the classic single or double strand of pearls. That's a perfect evening outfit for winter or summer.

A straight silk shift can make a terrific evening dress. So can a straight-cut tunic top in a good fabric—cotton, linen or silk—worn over evening pants.

When nothing else feels right, my old standby for evening is a pair of black linen or thin wool crepe pants, or a soft black skirt, short or long, worn with a white silk shirt and a knockout dressy belt. Add high-heeled black sandals that have a delicate look, or pale gold or silver sandals.

JEANS

Real ones. Good old-fashioned jeans in faded or not-so-faded denim. Good denim. I have worn jeans all my life. There is absolutely nothing new about them. They have been an important part of every wardrobe I have ever had. I always have a few pairs in my closet. I also have a couple of denim or blue-jean jackets. Sometimes they are exactly right. I wear jeans with all the types of shirts I have mentioned, including silk and ruffled shirts, as well as with sweaters and jackets. I wear them with running shoes, loafers or high heels. I wear them in New York City to go almost anywhere informally during the day. If it is warm, I often wear a cotton jacket or blazer with jeans, and in winter I wear them with tweed jackets and boots. *Vogue* ran a picture of me dressed just that way in 1978. The picture has been used many places. It shows me and a beautiful young girl running down a street in New York City. We are both wearing our own clothes. We had, just by chance, showed up for work dressed that way for a shooting called "Dressing in Four Ages." I was the oldest model and she was the youngest.

ACCESSORIES

A couple of soft, striped silk neckties, like men's but unstructured and designed for women. Ascots in cotton or silk with small patterns or prints. Silk or cotton neck scarves as well as the larger scarves that can be worn as kerchiefs over your hair or tucked into a coat or jacket front or tied beautifully about your neck and shoulders and accented by a small brooch or good-looking pin. These are always in my bureau drawers. Narrow belts in plain black, brown, taupe, red or navy leather with simple silver or gold buckles, plus one very dressy black belt with a gorgeous rhinestone buckle, are also within my reach year-round. And simple, basic jewelry.

SHOES

Jogging shoes, loafers, walking shoes and just plain simple pumps in medium and high heels in the basic colors. High-heeled black strap evening sandals, a pair of soft gold or silver pumps and gold or silver sandals with heels wait in my closet too—year-round.

A tank-style maillot bathing suit, a light windbreaker and a pair of shorts are there too in case of a trip.
One never knows.

Bridging the Seasons

I dress for cool-cold weather or warm-hot weather. Spring and fall clothes are, for the most part, accommodated by what I already have. I wear very much the same things in the fall as I do in the winter and I think most people do. A tweed jacket, a blazer or a cardigan sweater over a blouse, dress or another sweater will do in the fall. When the weather turns colder, I add a classic wool topcoat, coachman's or polo-style, or a wool-lined trench coat, a down coat or a fur coat, along with boots and the necessary accessories—warm gloves, hats, wool caps and scarves.

Each season, I might make a few additions to my wardrobe to make dressing more fun and interesting. They might be expensive, but they are lasting. For instance, a red cashmere cape with a hood that reaches to my knees and easily covers anything I wear underneath it, including heavy sweaters and jackets. It is gay and snappy; it works well with skirts or pants, high heels or flats and is superb with good-looking boots. Or a pair of light taupe chamois culottes, with enough material so the soft leather falls in folds and looks almost as though it were a skirt. I have worn this successfully far more often than I expected. While it really is a casual look, I found I could dress it up with a black sweater or the right jacket. It also works with either heels or boots. Expensive, yes. But elegant and, with care, even practical. I'll continue to enjoy it and wear it for years.

Both the cape and the culottes can be worn throughout the winter and in transition seasons. I have also used the cape as a blanket on long-distance plane flights, and as an extra cover when visiting or in a hotel. Cashmere is not tough to take. I sleep well in it.

A gabardine skirt in taupe, beige or soft brown; a pair of khaki pants; a pair of lightweight wool gray flannels; light-colored corduroy skirts and pants all help bridge the changing seasons in both fall and spring.

The season-spanning suits: A navy blue suit with a straight skirt and bolero jacket worn with a silk chemise top. A straight black wool worsted skirt and double-breasted blazer with smart gold buttons. The blazer works effectively with gray flannels, white cotton slacks, even blue jeans. These suits are perfect for business lunches, meetings, giving talks and for nearly any day or evening occasion except those that are very formal.

132

Winter and Summer Basics

The clothes that move in and out of my closet for winter and for summer are basics. For winter, a classic shirtwaist dress, a wool jumper and wool skirts, slacks, tweed jackets and solid-color blazers. The skirts and slacks are in neutral colors—camel, gray, taupe and black. They combine easily and well with the jackets, sweaters, blouses and shirts.

My winter jackets vary in length. The shorter ones work better with skirts. The very short, waist-fitting jacket is wonderful with a long, full skirt. Full skirts need fitted blouses, jackets or small sweaters, rather than something large and blousy that tends to make everything look too large, including you.

Longer jackets are better with pants. They should cover your derriere, not hit you midway. Large, loose and unstructured jackets, good for wearing over layers, are chic with a long narrow straight skirt or one with a slight A-line. A slit in a straight skirt makes walking easier and helps create the illusion of long legs. A slit in a straight skirt of any length is pretty sexy.

A black coat-dress with satin lapels and a velvet suit with a short skirt helps round out my winter wardrobe.

In summer, cotton skirts, structured and unstructured, lightweight cotton jackets, cotton pants, a pair of black linen and a pair of white linen slacks, wide white silk pants with a drawstring top, and a white linen slacks suit (again, the jacket can be used with other skirts and slacks) replace the winter wools.

Whether it's winter or summer, I am always turning up a collar to frame my neck and face, pushing a little bright scarf into a jacket breast pocket, making sure my shirt cuffs show beyond my jacket sleeves or turning up short sleeves instead of just letting them sit there in a blah fashion. In winter, textured silk or wool scarves add interest to any jacket, sweater or coat, particularly if they are worn with flair and a slight sense of abandon—not made to look rigid and stuck in place.

I have very few dresses because I find very few that work. Really work. Do something for me. Give something to me. Too many take away from me instead. The classic chemise, shift, jumper or shirtwaist dress is always good when the proportions are right for you. But many dresses lose their proportions when hems are taken up or let down. If you can't wear a dress the way it is, maybe it should be left out of your wardrobe. Check very carefully if you have to alter a hemline to see if the proportions still look right on you.

Simple is more. You are the event. Remember?

Style: The Look That Stays with You

I found my style and I stay with it. I just upgrade it as I grow older. It would be easy to suggest that it is a preppy type of dressing, but preppy is for kids and I am not a kid. I have some sophistication, which is one of the wonderful aspects of being an older woman, and my style reflects this whether I am in jeans or an evening dress. I like that a lot.

My daytime style has a menswear flair to it. What is that? To me, what is called man's-style dressing on women has absolutely nothing to do with gender. It is just a style. If it works, then it can be your style. Many women in this country are conditioned to think that clothing that "suggests" masculine is not feminine. Not true. Women are not *supposed to* dress in a certain way. There is no *supposed to*, any more than there is dressing a certain way because you are a certain age. There are only clothes that work for you and enhance your appearance, and clothes that don't.

I know my style is not every woman's style. Some women don't like pants and won't wear them, perhaps because of body structure and size. I am very aware of this. My mother struggled all her life with a weight problem. She was five feet three inches tall and weighed from 150 up to 190 pounds most of her adult life. She would never tell her exact weight. Whatever it was, she didn't like it. It controlled her dressing. She loved clothes and wanted to wear certain styles but never felt she could. She even felt she couldn't wear simple skirts and sweaters due to her build and weight. She was very short in the leg and very buxom. She was also very beautiful and always looked beautiful in what she did wear—usually dresses. Simple caftans, muumuus or dresses made for her with the right proportions. She would add soft chiffon scarves, some jewelry and would often have a cotton, silk or thin wool stole to put around her shoulders in the evening. She kept her dressing simple and refined. Heavy, yes. But thoroughly elegant. Always Beautiful.

Fashion

What is thought of as fashion today is for the most part instantaneous. Instantly here. Instantly gone. But style, good style, classic style, lasts and lasts. There should be at least some simple classic styles in every woman's closet. Every wardrobe needs that elegance, no matter how much it costs. Elegant clothes are the Rolls-Royces of dressing. They are beautiful and elegant whenever you take them out and wear them. Year after year after year.

The young girl who is working at dressing, working at being sexy and playing with instant fashion is a far cry from the woman who has her style and knows how to wear her clothes because she knows who and what she is.

She *is* sexy and *Always Beautiful*.

NURTURING
BEAUTY
NUTRITIONALLY

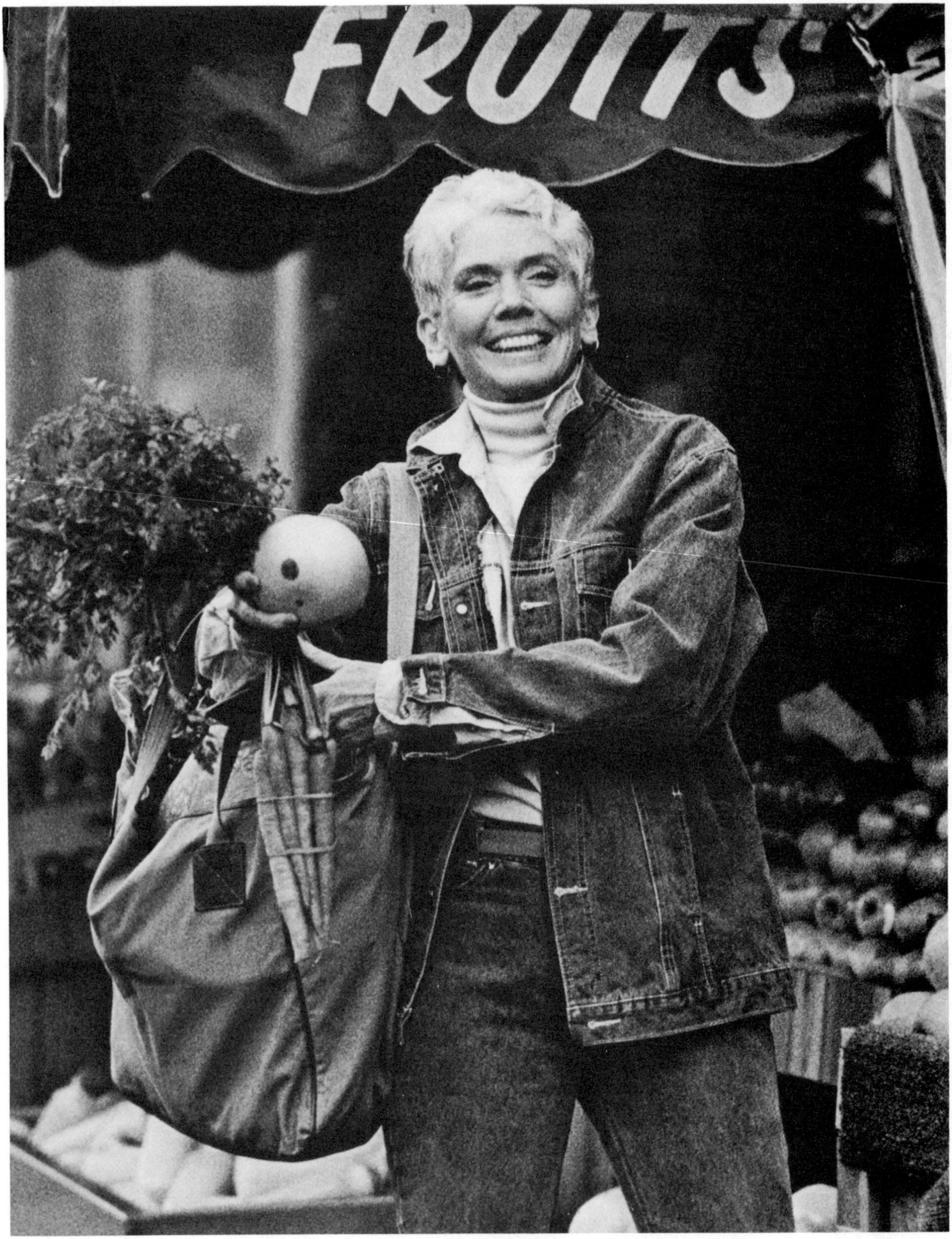
FRUITS

> You may measure yourself by size,
>
> weight and age, but live in
>
> beauty, spirit and love.

YOU are your most important challenge. The real effort you have to make is to know what is going on inside you: your feelings, actions and reactions. In other words, how you think of yourself. It is not easy work, but it is the most important work you can do, and it will help give definition and shape to your life. Literally.

We have to learn to listen to our thinking about ourselves. I've heard it, you've heard it:

"I don't know how this happened to me. It just did. I was thin all my life until—"

"I stopped smoking and immediately gained twenty pounds and—"

"Oh, God. It's always such a fight not to gain weight. Since the change—"

"To hell with it. I can't worry about it anymore. I'm fat and that's the way it is for me."

"At my age, it's no big deal that I'm overweight. Who gives a—"

Where do you put the blame? Pressure? Temptations? Age? Hormones? Boredom? Anger? Unused energy and creativity? Insufficient love? Fear? Resentment? Guilt? Self-dislike? I know and you know you can do something about it, but you have to *want* to.

If excessive weight provides emotional security, then you may want to stay that way. You don't have to be the weight that medicine says is right for your age, your body frame and your health. It's an option you have. But you also have the option to take control. You start exercising that option when you know and understand your behavior.

As truths surface, you will grow stronger and more confident. You will just plain feel better. And as your attitude toward yourself and your extra weight shifts to the better, you can gain the control you need to shift those excess pounds into oblivion.

The extent of overweight and bad nutrition in America is amazing. Are our bad eating habits culturally conditioned? Many studies have been done on nearly everything related to our health and nutrition. I doubt that we can blame all of the problem on culture, but some saddening statistics have recently surfaced:

- Nearly 35 percent of American men and nearly 50 percent of American women are overweight.
- Of the ten leading causes of death, six are connected to diet.
- A Congressional study suggests that only 10 to 20 percent of today's medical procedures are truly beneficial to us.
- Of all the medical schools in the United States, only 12 percent have complete and separate departments for the study of nutrition.
- Approximately 10 million Americans suffer from high blood pressure.
- Blood fats and cholesterol are not the same kind of fat as body fat. Reducing the amount of cholesterol you consume will not necessarily reduce fat in general or make you thinner.
- Forty to 50 percent of the calories consumed by Americans are fat calories without nutritional value.

You Have to Move Your Body to Lose Weight

Even though as Americans we consume fewer calories now than at the turn of the century, we are fatter. This is because we eat so much that is bad for us and have comparatively sedentary lifestyles.

One solution is to add more exercise to your life. Exercise speeds up the metabolic rate, forcing calories to be burned up faster. (To lose one pound of body fat, you have to burn up 3500 more calories than you consume.) Walking, biking, swimming or running even fifteen to twenty minutes a day will make a positive difference for you.

- If you do more physical exercise and eat fewer calories, you will lose weight.
- If you do exactly what you have been doing and eat fewer calories, you will lose weight.

- If you do more physical exercise and eat the same number of calories, you will lose weight.
- With no activity, calories will lodge in your cells and stay there!

Physical activity forces stored fat to move into your bloodstream to feed the working muscles. Then sugar is released by the liver to help this process. During activity and following it, fat cells shrink as the muscles burn their fuel (calories).

Your metabolism is high after eating because your system goes to work digesting food. Adding exercise during digestion (anywhere from a half hour to an hour after eating) may burn up even more calories, like adding another log on the fire to make it burn longer. The point is: Eat your big meals before an activity to burn up the most calories. You can see how skipping breakfast or eating a light breakfast, having a light lunch and then a big dinner works counter to this theory. To lose weight, you should do the reverse: Eat a large, nutritious breakfast, less for lunch and the least amount of food at night.

Some Diet Guidelines

What you need to eat varies with your age, sex, how active you are and how happy. Experts say that negative mental attitudes, stress, illness, and even intense emotions of happiness or sadness can change the body's chemistry so that nutrients are unable to work as efficiently or effectively.

Although a new fad diet appears every season, only 10 percent of all people who diet maintain weight loss. Often that is because crash dieting causes the body to lose water and lean muscle instead of fat.

A good diet should have variety and never have fewer than 1000 calories per day. It should be aimed at changing your eating habits permanently and educating your body to crave foods that are good for it.

And we do need serious education. The average American consumes approximately 130 pounds of sugar a year, and sugar has no nutritional value. In fact, excessive consumption of nonnutritive calories can sometimes create a hormonal deviation. Sugar raises blood sugar, which in turn raises energy level, releasing insulin into our system. Then it drops off sharply and we crash, hungry again. A connection has been made between too much sugar and faulty functioning of adrenal glands, hypertension, tooth decay, ulcers, diabetes, arteriosclerosis and heart disease.

Many of us were convinced that a high-protein diet was the healthiest, the one that made us strong. We were wrong. Protein not needed for energy can become fat. Too much protein can change your metabolism and generate weight gain. Excessive protein can also cause dehydration in the body and rob it of calcium as well as contribute to the exhaustion of the kidneys. What's more, diets high in protein have been linked with osteoporosis.

One gram of protein equals four calories. One gram of complex carbohydrates also equals four calories. And complex carbohydrates have become the diet good guys. They are an essential source of fiber, fuel and energy, yet they are not connected to any of the major diseases that kill us.

Complex carbohydrates—fruits, vegetables and grains—create approximately 20 to 25 percent of our diet, but they should comprise about 45 percent of it.

Getting Your Nutritional Balance

The major food categories that everyone needs to draw from to have a complete and wholesome diet are:

Complex carbohydrates: Fruits (natural sugar), vegetables, greens, cereals, whole-grain breads, wheat, corn, oats (unrefined).
Proteins: Lean meat, poultry, eggs, fish, dry peas and beans (legumes).
Dairy products: Milk, cheese, yogurt (all should be low-fat).

The complex carbohydrates that supply fiber make our digestive systems work harder, so fewer calories are stored away. Instead, they get burned up or blocked as they tangle with the tough fiber. Fiber foods are also high in bulk and fill you up faster than less nourishing foods, thus helping curb your appetite.

Today's nutritionists theorize that everyone should have two servings of fiber at each meal, not just one, and that fiber should be eaten for snacks in between meals. Aside from the fact that fiber foods are low in calories and supply us with the right kind, they are also believed to help prevent ailments like colon cancer, diverticula diseases, ulcers, hemorrhoids and even varicose veins.

Complex carbohydrates are not complicated. Eat garden plants, grains, use bran alone or with other foods and don't be afraid to eat potatoes, rice, pasta and fresh grain breads. These fiber-supplying foods are nutritious, low in fat and cholesterol (if you leave off butter or other fats) and supply energy.

Protein was at one time considered the essential ingredient for strength and energy, but researchers have discovered a connection between the high fat content of protein foods (such as red meat, whole dairy products and oils, particularly saturated or animal oils, like butter) and potentially killer diseases like cancer of the breast, colon and prostate. They also believe that certain processed meats, like salami and hot dogs, contain nitrates that are converted into carcinogenic nitrosamines in the body; stomach cancers have been on the decline in this country since people began eating less of these products.

Fortunately, protein is available in low-fat foods too, such as chicken (without skin), turkey (unprocessed) and most fish and shellfish. Protein can also be created by combining legumes—beans and peas—with grains like rice and wheat. Such combinations are used regularly by vegetarians to supply protein in their diet. It is suggested that everyone should eat approximately six ounces of protein daily.

Dairy products are an important source of nourishment if the fat has been skimmed off. Skim milk, low-fat yogurt and cottage cheese are dairy foods with low-fat content. They are also important sources of calcium. Two eight-ounce glasses of skim milk provide the recommended daily allowance of calcium.

Our intake of calcium and phosphorus should be balanced as much as possible: Protein foods contain more phosphorus than calcium, and dairy products have more calcium than phosphorus. While milk in any form is rich in calcium so are some fruits, like pineapples and oranges, and dark green leafy vegetables.

About 30 percent of the population doesn't get enough calcium through diet and needs to take calcium supplements. This is particularly true for women during and after menopause. Hormonal changes that a woman undergoes in menopause are now linked to the depletion of bone and osteoporosis. Calcium and exercise are strongly recommended as natural ways to slow down and control this problem. Calcium supplements combined with vitamin D are very important for the woman in mid-life and most specifically for the woman during and after menopause.

Calcium is also believed to be beneficial to our muscles, and helpful to people who suffer from arthritis. Diets that eliminate beef, sugar, white flour and other processed foods have also helped many arthritic patients.

New Thinking About Food

As a human being you were given a mind that can reason, contemplate and evaluate the state of your own physical life. If weight is a problem, you can reason how you want to handle it. You can choose a fast and easy way to lose weight by popping pills or starving yourself. No fun. But it doesn't demand thinking or self-examination, either. That sort of choice is unfortunate but understandable—for years you've just taken something for whatever ails you, rather than first trying to work with nature to understand what could be helpful and best for you.

With this same reasoning mind, you can also contemplate your physical decline and even your own death. It is true that as you grow older your body eventually becomes weaker and frail. But if you have paid positive attention to your life and have understood what your living has been about, your spirit will have grown stronger. Isn't that logical, since it is your spirit that moves on and not your body? The design is quite perfect.

You don't need to shorten your physical life span out of stupidity, ignorance, willfulness, indifference, gluttony, laziness or fear of honest personal investigation. The unwillingness to meet yourself. I'm learning new thinking about food. Like almost everyone I know, I need to understand and manage it creatively, in moderation and balance.

Again, since you are unique, you have to educate yourself to your body's needs. As you develop new awareness, you will become more sensitive to your reactions and will learn to recognize how much food is enough. You will know your own comfort zone and begin to respect it. You will also learn to see the times you take a dive for food, any kind of food, and why and how frequently. Depending on the degree of self-understanding you develop, you can learn to work with, not against, yourself.

Food serves your appetite and contributes to your life, so be especially aware of foods that are good for you. They are plentiful. You can be your own best expert with some thought and effort.

With new diet books being published every month and new health food counters springing up in supermarkets, we're becoming more conscious than ever before of what we eat and that we should eat well. Then why is it so many of us still load the supermarket carts with colas, chips and sugary desserts?

As I travel around the country, I see that the majority of women over forty are also overweight. Sometimes I think it is because we would rather feed our psyches than our bodies. If we could think of ourselves as prize-winning biological specimens, deserving only the best-quality nourishment, we would be conditioned to avoid junk foods, sugary snacks and sodas. But we have grown up with certain "comfort foods" that we associate with relaxation, good times, love and family. And now, during mid-life, one of life's transition periods, we need them psychologically.

So it becomes apparent: You have to reeducate yourself to find *new comfort foods*. You have to consider indulging yourself, pampering yourself with foods that are as fresh as possible—top-quality nutrients. You're worth it.

First, you must take charge of what you eat. Confront your unhealthy eating habits head-on. Face up to them.

Know Thy Eating Habits

Here is a technique used by many of New York's top nutritional counselors, and it's one sure way to come to terms with your nutritional needs. Make a chart of your day, dividing it into hourly periods along one side of the paper. Then make two columns, one headed "Foods Eaten" and another headed "Moods." Keep this chart nearby and record everything you eat and drink. Every cup of coffee, every potato chip, every glass of water or soda. Photocopy the original chart and fill out one every day for a week. Under "Moods," write down how you were feeling at the time—nervous, happy, tense, frustrated, hurried. And how hungry you were.

At the end of the week you should have a fairly good picture of your eating habits and how you feel (besides hungry) at the times you choose to eat. If you don't already know the troublemakers in your diet, you should be able to pinpoint them, as well as the times of day when you crave sugar, how much coffee you really drink, how much alcohol, how much protein and fiber you consume. Remember, from here on in you're in charge of your diet. Make up your mind that you are going to feed your body, not your psyche.

Eat Fresh and in Season

Fresh seasonal foods are the foods of beauty. Splurge on freshness! Learn to enjoy fresh fruits and vegetables, as close to their natural state as possible. Find the best produce market in your neighborhood and discover the wonderful range of fresh vegetables and fruits. Forget boring iceberg lettuce that seems to cry out for creamy dressings. Instead, spice up your salads with peppery arugula, watercress, red lettuce, tiny straw mushrooms, fresh basil. You'll never say "rabbit food" again. A dressing of high-quality salad oil and lemon or vinegar will be all you need.

Cut Down on Cooking

When it comes to cooking for health and beauty, the less you do the better. Foods eaten close to their natural state retain all of their nutrients. If you live in a part of the country where people routinely overcook their vegetables, it is important to overcome this habit.

Here are some kitchen appliances that can help you form new eating habits:

A wok: Stir-fry cooking (not to be confused with deep-fat frying) in a wok is one of the healthiest ways to prepare meals. The food is cooked or steamed in a small amount of oil. It cooks very rapidly and emerges crisp and crunchy.

A juice extractor: You can get concentrated nutrients and enzymes from large amounts of vegetables quickly and easily. Try combinations of carrot, beet, celery, cucumber and watercress juice. If you don't eat enough vegetables, this is a great way to remedy the situation. Make it a habit to have a glass of vegetable juice every day.

A blender: You can make instant nutritious drinks and purees and low-calorie dips for raw vegetables. Or whip up an instant breakfast of a raw egg, banana, honey and yogurt, or yogurt and orange juice. Substitute strawberries, peaches, oranges—whatever you like. Add brewer's yeast, protein powder or granular lecithin. It's fast, it's easy and it's far more nutritious than coffee and a Danish. Experiment with smooth, spicy dips using avocado, yogurt, garlic, fresh herbs. These will make raw vegetable snacks more interesting and give you an outlet for culinary creativity.

A vegetable steamer: These little gadgets, which sell for under five dollars, could change the way you cook your vegetables forever. Instead of boiling them to death in water, thus removing all their vitamins, you just slip this perforated stainless-steel sieve into a saucepan with a little water in the bottom and cover. Your vegetables will cook to just the right crispness in several minutes.

Add These Foods to Your Diet

These are protective, preventive foods, especially rich in nutrients and vitamins. They're foods that work for you. They should be in your diet all year round.

Bananas: High in potassim, vitamin B6 and biotin (also of the B family).

Beans: Lower cholesterol and triglyceride levels. Also contain B vitamins, iron and magnesium.

Bran: Important for fiber. Add to breakfast cereals, muffins, breads. Corn bran is 90 percent fiber; wheat bran is 50 percent fiber. Oat bran has been found to lower cholesterol.

Cabbage, Broccoli, Brussels sprouts: High in vitamins A and C, calcium and potassium. These vegetables act as detoxifiers and protect against cancer.

Carrots: High in beta-carotene and fiber. Low in calories.

Citrus fruits: Contain vitamins A, C and E as well as pectin fiber. The combined effects of these vitamins are believed to help prevent cancer.

Fish: Some fish, like salmon, help lower blood pressure and triglycerides.

Garlic and onions: Considered blood purifiers and cleansers. Help fight cholesterol.

Leafy greens: High in vitamin A and calcium and contain chlorophyll, which is thought to fight cancer.

Liver: Contains nearly all essential nutrients, including zinc, iron and copper. Contains vitamins A, E, K and B12, also thiamine, riboflavin, biotin, choline and inositol.

Melons: Low in calories and high in vitamin C.

Nuts: High in zinc, but can also be high in calories. Almonds are high in trace minerals.

Peppers (red and green): High in vitamin C. Red peppers are also high in vitamin A.

Poultry: High in nutrients and low in calories.

Seeds: May have cancer-fighting properties. Pumpkin, sesame and sunflower seeds are high in zinc and protein.

Soy products: Soybeans, tofu and miso. High in protein, help lower cholesterol, thought to protect against cancer.

Sprouts: High in magnesium, calcium and vitamin C. A great year-round "live" food.

Sweet potatoes: High in vitamin A, low in calories. Vitamin A is believed to be helpful against cancer.

Wheat germ: Contains B vitamins and thiamine and can be used with many other foods.

Whole grains: Breads, cereals and brown rice all contain fiber and help lower cholesterol and fight cancer.

Yogurt: Easily digestible, helps lower cholesterol, high in calcium and protein.

Make Your Food Look Beautiful

Make your foods a feast for the eyes, especially if you're eating less. Use your best china and silver. Serve your fruit and vegetable juices in beautiful crystal glasses. Too often we save our best china and silver for ceremonious occasions. Why not enjoy their beauty every day? Make your dining experience as beautiful as possible with lovely colored place mats, your favorite dishes and glassware. Meals are to be enjoyed visually, too.

Remember, You're Not Alone!

If you have a serious weight problem, you are very much in need of psychological support while you revamp your body chemistry. It's an excellent idea to consult a nutritionist to get a diet designed especially for your body's needs. This could involve blood tests, hair analysis, and constant weight monitoring. But, if you do have a drastic weight problem, expert help is in order. More and more patients are also prevention-oriented, and doctors are becoming aware of the value of good nutrition and are prepared to give you more specific advice than "just eat a balanced diet."

If you're not a loner, find a "diet buddy." You can reinforce each other, exercise together, give each other praise and encouragement. And, when you've lost weight, you have someone to really celebrate with.

Another possibility: Join a weight-loss club. Here you'll find a host of new friends, all in the same boat. Many clubs, such as Weight Watchers, have nutritionally approved meal plans to follow. However, be very careful of liquid-protein diets or powdered diet plans, on which you eat only liquid or powder preparations. Fasting, too, should be done only under the strictest supervision.

I would also beware of diet pills, diuretics and appetite suppressants. You should be after long-term results for your health, not just short-term gains.

Many so-called diet aids contain substances that overstimulate the body, and then throw its chemistry off balance.

It's far better to lose gradually and keep your weight off than to go for the "lost ten pounds in one week" hype, where you'll lose mostly water and balloon right up again in no time. There is nothing more discouraging than yo-yo dieting. So think in terms of a lifetime eating plan, and keep those pounds off for good.

Eat Less, Exercise More!

When your body stays at the same weight for a long period of time it tends to "settle" at that weight, becoming comfortable and resisting change unless you alter your diet and exercise habits. It's important that your body's comfort and your mental and emotional comfort about your body agree.

While there seems to be little doubt that some people's metabolism is more sluggish than others, nearly everyone's metabolism slows down as they grow older. So, like it or not, you probably need to eat less and exercise more to keep weight from slowly piling up. Certainly, you need to exercise more if you haven't been doing any at all.

The Controversial Foods

It is not news today that people who choose to live on processed foods and products loaded with white flour and refined sugar (which are also frequently loaded with fats and contain no nutritional value) are courting health problems—problems that may not become apparent for years. Your hard-working cells can be abused by being undernourished for just so long before they protest.

Cholesterol is still a subject of controversy, but we do know some things for certain. Cholesterol is made in our bodies and we also ingest it from foods like meat, dairy products and eggs. Too much cholesterol (a state generally created by our dietary habits) causes fat deposits in blood vessels, which contribute to heart attacks. Animal or saturated fats are known to create higher levels of cholesterol in the blood, while fats from vegetable and fish products, known as polyunsaturated fats, lower cholesterol in the blood. The type of fat found in some nuts is thought to be harmless and beneficial.

149

Sugar calories are frequently referred to as dense calories, which have no nutritive value. The danger from sugar-dense calories comes not just from refined white sugar, but also from brown sugar and sugar syrups like molasses, corn and maple. The experts are still arguing about honey. Some say yea; others say nay. My own feeling is that a little won't hurt, but then I probably want to think that because I like it. Fruits, on the other hand, give us a natural form of sugar that helps clear toxins from our systems and supplies nourishment to our cells.

Salt is dangerous for a very well-known reason: it encourages high blood pressure. Nutritionists caution us not to add salt to our food because in a balanced diet you will get enough of it from foods that already contain sodium. A gram a day is sufficient.

Coffee is generally thought to be a poor addition to our diet. Some doctors and nutritionists do not equivocate at all and say that it is absolutely bad for us because of the caffeine, which is found in tea, chocolate, cocoa and the cola drinks as well. Caffeine can cause jitters, stomach problems and irritation, heart palpitations, elevated blood pressure that then drops suddenly. It is also now associated with fibrocystic breast disease and cancer of the bladder. And to add insult to injury, coffee contains no nutrients.

Sodas contain sugar and phosphoric acid, which is capable of dissolving tooth enamel. Granted, you would have to consume outrageous amounts of soda to lose tooth enamel, but the point is obvious: it's neither good nor helpful for you.

Water is essential to LIFE. Since our bodies contain such a high percentage of water, it is vital to keep fluids moving through our systems. Water helps flush toxins, waste material and mucus from the body. It also increases the movement of oxygen and nutrients in our blood supply and, last but not least, keeps our inner machinery lubricated and safe from dehydration.

We should drink six to eight glasses of water each day, and more when we exercise. A well-watered system can even make weight loss easier; when you keep the pump primed, water flows out faster.

There is disagreement on what sort of water to drink. Some nutritionists say you should drink only bottled mineral water. Some say only sparkling water or low-sodium sparkling or mineral water. Certainly check the sodium content if you buy any type of bottled water. Others argue that all water contains minerals, not just mineral waters. I think everyone is aware that our tap water supply is loaded with chemicals put there to keep it safe for drinking (and free from the other chemicals that pollute the earth and air). Around and around we go. It is a terrible irony.

It is important to read labels on packaged foods today so you have some idea of what you may ingest. It is particularly important for anyone who is ood- or allergy-sensitive to check labels for dyes, additives and other chemicals.

Food processors may not be ecstatic about releasing information and warnings to the public as researchers uncover negative food facts. But neither is the public ecstatic. What we are learning is bewildering, but the picture is clear in at least several respects. Natural foods are better for us; fresh foods are better for us; food that is uncontaminated by chemicals is better for us.

Finding where to buy the right foods takes extra time and effort, unless you grow your own or live in the country and know where it is available. We, myself included, are too often inclined to be lazy, and we have learned to accept unnatural foods, to our detriment. We have learned to like a lot of them—and I include myself again. But I am learning to eat well, to eat foods that work for me and that will keep me healthy and beautiful. So can you.

EXERCISE
FOR
YOUR LIFE

Romance, love and sex . . .

Do they desert you, or you

them? They are beauty too.

YOUR thoughts about yourself are not arbitrary—you create them. Whether they are positive or negative, you can use them as keys to unlock a greater sensitivity to what your body needs to be its healthy, beautiful best.

Because you are always evolving, it is important to keep up with your changing self, particularly your physical changes. You may need to develop new thinking about your body. You may need to become aware of the unique way your body has developed and what your prospects are for being a beautiful woman now and in the future.

But first you have got to get rid of some heavy mental baggage. I mean having the attitude that beauty talk does not apply to you. Many women exempt themselves from taking the proper concern for their bodies by constantly reaffirming feelings like "I'm over the hill"; "No matter what I do, I'll never be beautiful"; or how about "I can't afford it. It's too expensive and time-consuming." The average American woman today can get her body to the point where she is truly satisfied with it. You don't have to be rich or young to do this; you simply must want to look and feel the best you can.

Then you have to literally give yourself permission to pay positive attention to yourself. Throw away the mental baggage that says it's selfish, it's expensive, it's hopeless. Attitudes like those provide a very poor basis for living the rest of your life.

Next, you need to make a commitment. A commitment to yourself, not to an exercise mat, a cosmetics box or a diet book. Those are just tools. The commitment is to you.

Decide to Be Beautiful

Ever notice how when you're in love you "grow" beautiful? It's because somewhere inside, you insist, you decide to be beautiful. A woman who feels beautiful and loved can radiate beauty. She sends out positive vibes that attract others.

You have to know who and what you are and claim beauty for yourself. Even when you are in fantastic physical shape and groom yourself beautifully, you can't just sit around and wait for outside approval from a man or from society. Staying locked into a negative self-appraisal will not help you achieve anything, including (and especially) attracting a man. If you, like thousands upon thousands of women, have sublimated your sexual needs because you think sex is out of the question for you, or not important, or unseemly at your time of life, or you have been hurt and are afraid to get involved again (or think no one would want you), or it's been so long you've forgotten, or it just doesn't matter—think again! Where have you put your passionate self? If all that energy is squelched and suppressed, you are working against, not for, yourself. Your energies need to be channeled creatively, and they include your sexual energies as well as the effort you put into work you love.

We are at our sensual and sexual best in our maturity—in mid-life—when we know who we are. That's beauty.

Care About Yourself!

Women often ask—no, *tell*—me that I must be a very disciplined person because I seem to stay in shape and lead a fairly demanding life. I can only answer both yes and no. Yes, I am organized. But no, I'm not disciplined in the way most people think of discipline. Discipline is not something I regretfully impose upon myself in order to do my work. I do what I love to do, and I know that if I don't have enough self-respect to take care of myself physically, nothing will happen and I won't achieve anything for very long.

The ingredient that is easy to overlook is love. It's not a question of discipline, it's a matter of desire. Caring. It is important that you learn what is essential for your happiness and health so your natural beauty—yes, your natural beauty—grows.

Selectivity and Simplicity: Goals for Your Start-up Exercise Program

I am frequently asked, How do I *keep* my shape? How do I control my weight? What sort of diet do I use? Do I take supplements? Vitamins? What sort of exercise do I do? In other words, how come I look good at my age?

You may think age is *the* criterion. I don't.

One way I help myself is by not allowing myself to be overwhelmed by too much information. No one can try every exercise or diet she hears about. *Selectivity becomes important.* The more complex society becomes, the more I want to control my own life. I can do this only by choosing to fulfill my own needs, not other people's desires for me. My own for myself!

I look for simplicity. I want my exercises to be manageable and usable, otherwise I defeat myself from the start. It is so easy to find reasons not to do something, and it is particularly easy if what you are trying to do is complicated. Keep it simple.

A simple exercise routine also gives me independence. I have to know that I can exercise by myself, that I can take care of myself wherever I go. Sometimes it is fun to work out with a group or in a fitness and exercise club, but that is not always possible or even desirable. And for hundreds of thousands of women it is not affordable. I want the freedom not to have to go somewhere special to exercise (and I exercise that freedom often).

Really, you don't *need* a class or a gym. Nature gave you everything you need to take care of yourself. You need use only what you were given. You can stretch or flex your muscles. You can walk. You know how to run or jog. Most people can swim, ride a bike or even jump rope. There is nothing mysterious, new or original about what I do. Or, for that matter, what thousands of other mid-life women who are in wonderful shape do.

Getting Back to the Basics

Today, science recognizes that many of our illnesses can be traced to our own thinking and to negative, self-defeating self-programming. Those negative feelings tend to pile up, particularly if you are contemplating an out-of-shape mid-life body.

The truth is that people spend most of their lives denying their bodies, finding reasons to dislike or be ashamed of them, or just taking them for granted and treating them as if they were poor shacks instead of houses for the spirit. What do you think your spirit wants and needs in its house? You know!

Everyone knows what it's like to feel free from physical and mental problems. You feel *whole*. "Holy" comes from that word. They share a common root, just as your physical and spiritual selves are bound together and share you from your beginning. A direct way to feel whole is to work on the basics that nature demands: sufficient rest, balanced diet, adequate exercise.

Listen. My number-one exercise for all women is to use their ears. Listen to your own words about yourself and the way your body looks. If you are saying harsh, demeaning things about your body or yourself, stop! If you are stiff, overweight, arthritic, out of shape with weak muscles, your body is telling you something.

Next, move. I'm yelling this: Move your body! There is no way around this for either your health or your looks. You have to move to keep your body flexible, toned and fed with energy. If you keep your body moving, you will never have to feel old. You don't have to exercise the way a twenty- or thirty-year-old might. You are not trying to *be* that; you are trying to have the best of the next half of your life. And you can have the best. Consider the exercise you do as *preventive and preservative*.

Exercising for the Right Reasons

Most women decide to exercise for beauty reasons: to lose weight and firm up. Comparatively few exercise because it makes them feel good. Unfortunately, most women consider exercise a time-consuming and bothersome discomfort in their lives. They need an immediate reason to force them to do it.

If weight is the reason, it is a good enough one for starters. We are now realizing that most diets do not work in the long run and can even make matters worse, particularly the very low-calorie crash diets that force loss of water and valuable body protein. Body fat, which you really need to lose, demands twice as much exercise to achieve loss as protein. And losing it is difficult.

Your body responds automatically and protectively to the violent food alterations of a crash diet. Your cells reduce their activity to stave off what they read as a threat of starvation. This reduces the rate of calorie consumption. So when you crash-diet, you burn fewer calories than you would normally. You then put your body through yet another trauma when you decide that the diet is over and suddenly return to your regular eating habits. This process of slowing down, then speeding up your metabolism can cause you to gain more weight than when you started in the first place. Round and round you go.

On the other hand, your body has an automatic positive response to exercise. If you become physically active and maintain normal eating patterns, your body will monitor and adjust the balance of calories coming in to calories going out or being expended. But to activate this process, you have to go into action.

An active person can consume as many as five or six hundred more calories per day than an inactive person and stay much thinner. Once your body machinery is stimulated by exercise, it will continue to burn off calories for ten to fifteen hours after you have stopped. So if you exercise both in the morning and in the afternoon, you can get round-the-clock calorie-burning benefits.

Here are some other great things exercise can do:

Keep you from shrinking. Exercise helps you fight the pull of gravity on your skeleton, which causes it to stoop and curve when bone and muscle weaken with age. It is a known scientific fact that people between the ages of thirty and seventy-five shrink in height anywhere from one to three inches. This doesn't have to happen. Proper body alignment, a flexible spine and good muscle tone can prevent this crumpling.

Slow down osteoporosis. Exercise helps the problem of bone loss during and after menopause. It is one of the few remedies for this serious problem, which too often results in bone fractures in elderly women.

Speed up a sluggish metabolism. This is particularly important for the person in mid-life, when the metabolism slows down. A sluggish metabolism means almost automatic weight gain because you no longer burn up the same number of calories at the same rate as in earlier years.

Burn off the most calories. You'll burn up the most calories from a meal if you walk for twenty minutes, starting thirty minutes to an hour after your meal, when the digestive process is working.

Burn off body fat. Exercise generates energy that burns up body fat, not important muscle protein. The more muscle tissue you have, the better, since it burns calories more efficiently than fat tissue. With muscles, you either use them or lose them!

Reduce hunger and relieve tension. Exercise releases our stored natural tranquilizer beta-endorphin into the body system.

Help your heart. Exercise increases your heart's pumping ability, lowers

159

blood pressure, steadies the heart rate. All this in turn improves body tissues, aids breathing and lungs with increased oxygen and increases muscle in proportion to fat.

Have I convinced you that exercise *must* become a routine part of your life, not just something you do to lose weight or inches? You must do more than you are used to doing. If you want to get results—a trimmer, firmer, healthier body—your muscles must be moved to the point of exhaustion and then some. It is a building process. Anyone at any age can redefine muscle, but you can't give shape to fat.

There is no age limit to exercise. Even a very old body will respond. Remember, the billions of cells that make up your body are *living cells*, and they are trying to work for you, not against you. Help them with positive, nourishing thoughts and actions.

Exercise Your Options

As your concept of exercise widens to include the enormous variety of possible alternatives, exercising can become a game. You can be inventive with your program.

Obviously, you shouldn't dive into gymnastics or advanced yoga or hours of aerobics if you have done nothing physical for years. You must proceed slowly and build steadily and consistently, even if it takes a long time to arrive at your goal. Add one more step per day—do one more stretch than you did the day before. It is a beginning. The next day add two, then three. And so on. Those added movements can lead you to a new life, as well as a new look.

In the beginning, I found it helpful not to make endless new rules about how much, how long or even where I would exercise. But I made one major determination: that I would exercise each day. I began to find new ways to include it. This is not as good as a set routine and carefully worked-out program, but it is a beginning, and it helps develop your interest and enthusiasm without creating feelings of failure if you don't do the same thing each day.

My schedule is never the same any two days in a row. I know there will be days when I don't have time to walk as much as I would like to. Or because of an early morning modeling call, I may have to cut short my time for exercise at home. But I always know that I will replace one activity with another and vary what I do throughout the day. So can you.

I know I need to stretch my body each day to keep it supple and flexible. I know I also need to strengthen my muscles to build and maintain sound support for my skeletal frame and to build endurance. Every day I am sure to do several basic stretching exercises, isometric exercises that can be done anywhere, and some form of aerobic exercise for a fifteen- or twenty-minute period. The most helpful aerobic exercises are those that produce continuous movement in the major muscle groups of the body: Walking, jogging, trampoline jumping, cycling (on a stationary bike), swimming, roller-skating, aerobic dancing or jumping rope are all excellent. Light weight lifting, using three- to five-pound dumbbells, helps me tone muscles, making them firm and smoothly defined rather than just flabby. It will not make them bulge.

To get the most benefit from the exercises you choose, you must remember these fundamentals:

Correct body alignment. Look at people in mid-life and older who stand as tall as their height allows. They move with ease and grace, and you probably don't even think about whether they have lines in their faces. They do not suggest age. Instead, they suggest vibrant life. People who slouch, hunch or slump can seem very old, even if they are chronologically young.

Correct breathing. When you do your exercises, don't hold your breath, breathe! Correct breathing comes in and out from your stomach, not just up and down. You breathe correctly, automatically, in your sleep. When you are lying down flat, study your breathing and become conscious of exactly how it works so you will be sure to duplicate this action during your exercises. When you stretch, contract a muscle or reach, exhale. When you release or relax, inhale.

Correct abdomen and shoulder position. Your shoulders should be very relaxed, pulled back and down. Let them fall back and down naturally, not in the "West Point on parade" look. Your abdomen is a key point. It is the central support system for the body, the focal point that determines your balance and your ease of movement. The muscles of the abdomen are among the most crucial in your body and should be kept as strong and toned as possible to keep your back supported, your posture straight and your body in correct alignment. Unfortunately, abdominal muscles aren't used enough in our daily activities and tend to grow weak and sag. This in turn forces our back muscles to carry an unhealthy overload. They are literally trying to hold us up without help or support. This was not meant to be. When your abdominals are weak, back problems are sure to follow, along with a sense of weakness, even fatigue.

Exercise Is a Good Form of Stress

Stress has to be applied to the body in physical exercise to get results. The three most important types of exercise—stretching, isometrics and aerobics—involve different types of stress.

Stretching produces flexibility by increasing the degree of mobility in areas related to or connected with the body's joints. Stretching exercises should always be done in a smooth, flowing motion. Never force your body by straining or bouncing during a stretch. Just reach as far as you can and hold that position for a count of ten seconds, remembering to breathe deeply and evenly—inhale, exhale—all the time. You will find you can hold a stretch or any exercise better if you breathe, because your muscles need the oxygen.

Remember, too, that early in the morning your muscles are tighter than later in the day when they are stretched out from normal activity. Muscles always tighten when they are not used. They are also tighter in cold, dry air than in warm, moist air, which allows them to be more elastic.

Isometric exercises pit one muscle against another; holding and sustaining pressure at the point of resistance is what does the work. You use the body's natural resistance rather than that of a weight or a pulley, for instance. Isometrics are great exercises to do in sneaky places: waiting rooms, bank lines, offices, airplanes, anyplace you have time to kill. Every woman should have a repertoire of isometrics for every part of her body, to keep handy for just these times.

Aerobic exercise promotes the supply of oxygen in the system, stressing the body through repetition, speed and continuing muscle action. As you increase your pace to a new level, you speed up your heartbeat. This type of exercise involves high oxygen consumption. Low oxygen consumption exercises are best for building muscles because they use most of your body strength to sustain an activity (such as lifting a weight) as you gradually increase the number of repetitions and speed is not particularly important.

Not All Exercises Are Right for You

You have to be cautious and know your body's limitations when choosing your exercises, especially if you have not been exercising regularly. For instance:

Push-ups can narrow blood vessels and reduce circulation. They can be dangerous for people with high blood pressure. Instead, do a modified push-up by leaning against a wall, or if you are stronger, do a push-up from bended knees rather than from the feet.

Touching toes with straight legs is bad for your knees, forcing them to over-extend themselves and placing pressure on the lumbar vertebrae.

Deep knee bends can cause injury to the knee joints and are now considered dangerous. The suggested alternative is a half knee bend.

Sit-ups put pressure on the spinal column, which can cause lower back problems. Try sit-ups with the knees bent, feet on the floor. Or curl-ups, where you slowly roll up, vertebra by vertebra, holding on to your thighs.

Leg lifts can strain the lower back. Have an exercise instructor position you. You can do front leg lifts from a seated position. The no-no is a double leg lift done while lying on your back (which is commonly used to strengthen abdominals).

Extreme back arches or swayback positions cause stress. When possible, keep a flat or straight back.

Headstands and shoulder stands can strain the neck and back muscles, and can throw a body out of proper alignment if muscles are not very strong.

Jogging or running can cause many problems with your feet, legs, knees and back. If jogging is for you, then be sure to invest in the best shoes with proper support. Roughly two-thirds of every thousand serious joggers say they have sustained injuries at some time as a result of jogging.

Inversion boots enable you to hang upside down, reversing the pull of gravity and stretching your spine. However, they can be dangerous for people with high blood pressure or glaucoma, because blood suddenly collects in new and different areas, causing pressure. Five minutes is enough for anyone using inversion boots—and be sure to have someone nearby to help.

Exercise and Your Appetite

Since I am well entrenched in mid-life, I have developed the tendency to gain a fast five pounds and not be able to lose it easily. What mid-life woman is not familiar with that problem? When I gain weight, it now goes directly to my waist, abdomen, hips, thighs and behind. Since all women carry an additional layer of fat in these areas, the extra weight can persist with a vengeance, particularly when hormones diminish during menopause.

Unfortunately, this comes at a time of life when you are inclined to eat more and exercise less, even though the exact opposite should be your goal.

Exercise will help you out by actually decreasing your appetite. It challenges your body to stay fit and in shape. The shape you want. But you have to work with your entire body—there is no such thing as successful spot-reducing. If there were, I'd be the first to go for it! Your whole body should be involved, your whole metabolism, your whole frame and all your muscles. All of you. It's a myth that the more you exercise, the hungrier you get!

Your Exercise Schedule

I chose a potpourri of exercises from the three categories of stretching, isometrics and aerobics. I learned some of them in various classes I no longer attend. Like many women, I have joined and unjoined health clubs, swimming clubs and exercise clubs. Other exercises I seem to have known all my life, and still more came from books and magazines.

After putting all these exercise experiences together selectively, I decided that I would exercise each day, even if I never left my small studio apartment. I have learned how to be on my own.

Good and sufficient exercise can be done almost anywhere. You need very little space to do some warm-ups, stretching and isometrics and many of the aerobic exercises.

1. Warm up your body before you begin. About five to ten minutes of walking, jogging, jumping gently up and down will get the blood moving.
2. Spend ten to fifteen minutes doing stretches and isometrics.
3. Spend fifteen to thirty minutes on aerobic exercise. It can be a different one every day.
4. Spend the final five to ten minutes cooling down.

Another way to exercise is to alternate aerobics with stretching exercises. Do two or three minutes of aerobics (depending on your condition), then stretch for a minute or two, then back to the aerobics. Keep alternating.

The following exercises are the ones I use. I do some but not all of them every day, varying my routine so I don't get bored. They consist of stretching and isometrics and can be done easily. Many of them, particularly the isometrics, can be slipped in during daily activities, even done at an office desk.

Choose from these exercises and add your own. They are tools to help you program yourself in a way that suits your needs and your way of life. But remember, *take responsibility for yourself. That is the only way you will persist—when you answer to you.*

BREATHE CORRECTLY

A breathing exercise: Sit up straight. Do not lean on anything. Relax your stomach muscles. Begin to inhale. Your stomach will *expand*. The idea is to fill your abdomen, bringing the air into your chest. Feel the air moving into and filling up the lung cavity, expanding your rib cage. Fill your lungs to the top. Hold your breath for a second or two and then begin to exhale slowly through your nose. Do not exhale all at once. When you think all your breath is out, relax your rib cage and begin to pull in your abdomen in short jerks. This will release the remaining air. Practice this for a few minutes each day.

TO RELAX AND STRETCH THE NECK MUSCLES

1. Slowly rotate your head three times to the right and three times to the left. Keep your shoulders down to feel the stretch along the muscles on the sides of the neck.

2. Keeping your shoulders straight and down, drop your chin toward your chest. Turn your head slowly to the right as far as possible, as though to look over your shoulder. Turn your head to your left shoulder and back to center. Push your chin down to your chest. Repeat three times.

FOR THE NECK AND SHOULDERS

1. Lock your hands behind your head. Move your elbows forward, almost touching in front, resisting by pushing your head against your hands. Then open your elbows out to your shoulders like wings. Hold. Repeat five times.

2. Lock your hands behind your head. Press forward with your hands and back with your head. Hold. Repeat three times.

3. Place your right palm on the side of your face. Press. Resist with your head. Repeat with the left palm. Do this three times.

FOR THE SHOULDERS AND ARMS

1. Sitting or standing, lift your shoulders up straight toward your ears. Rotate them forward, down and back up in a circular motion. Repeat five times. (This exercise can be done moving both shoulders together or alternating one at a time.) Reverse the rotation of your shoulders, moving them in a circular motion toward your back. Repeat five times.

2. Bring your shoulders straight up toward your ears, as high as you can. Drop them down as far as you can. Repeat five times.

3. Bend your arms at the elbows and touch your collarbone with your fingers. Rotate your elbows, making circles, five forward, five backward. Increase to at least ten rotations in each direction. Good for circulation to head and neck area.

4. With arms straight out to the sides, flex your hands, fingers pointing up. Rotate your arms in small circles, graduating to larger ones. Do five or ten forward and the same number backward.

5. Raise both arms above your head. Clench your fists tightly. Stretch as high as possible. Hold. Release. Do five times.

6. Grasp one hand with the other behind your back. Press down as hard as you can. Hold. Repeat three to five times.

7. With your arms at your sides, make fists with both hands. Rotate your wrists in a circular motion to the left and right. Do five to ten times in each direction.

8. With your arms at your sides, stretch out all ten fingers on each hand. Then clench your fists. Then stretch out again as far as you can. Do this rapidly ten to twenty times.

FOR THE WAISTLINE

1. Sit on the floor. Bend at the waist and reach forward, slowly moving your hands down your legs to the point of strain. Hold. Release. Repeat three times.

2   3

2. Holding both arms straight above your head, reach high with your right
arm, then with the left, alternating short stretches right and left in a "fruit
picking" motion. Then go up and down on alternate toes as you pick. Do
this ten to twenty times to stretch the muscles from the waist through the rib
cage.

3. Stand with your legs hip width apart and your hands on your hips. Lean
to the left and bring your right arm over your head. Reach as far to the side
as you can, but keep your right hip down so you feel the stretch all along the
right side. Hold the stretch, then repeat on the opposite side. Do three to five
times on each side, alternating sides.

4. Bend at the waist. Flex knees. Drop head and arms straight in front of you. When you begin to feel a pull at the back of the thighs stop. Hold for six to ten seconds.

5. Sit on the floor, legs straight out in front of you. Place your right hand on your left knee and twist your body slowly to the left side as far as possible. Reverse sides. Repeat three times on each side.

4

5

FOR THE BACK AND ABDOMEN

1. Lie on the floor on your back with legs straight, arms out to the sides. With your head, hands and heels on the floor, tighten your buttock muscles and, pushing up with the pelvis, raise your buttocks off the floor. Hold for three seconds and relax. Lower your buttocks from the waist down, vertebra by vertebra. Relax. Repeat twice.

2. Lie on the floor on your back. Exhale. Pull in and up with your stomach, trying to flatten your spine against the floor. Hold. Repeat three times.

3. Lie on the floor on your back. Pull your knees toward your chest. Wrap

169

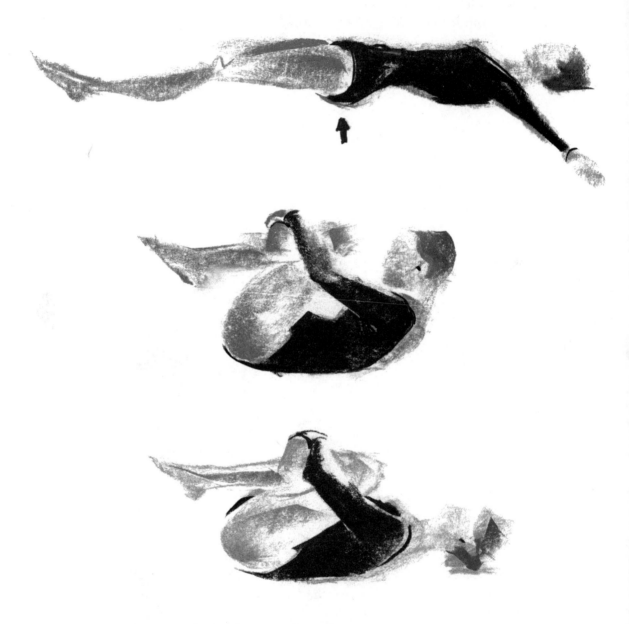

your arms around your knees and gently pull them down toward your chest to the point of strain. Hold for a count of six to ten. Relax.

4. You need an exercise mat or a thick rug for this one. Repeat the previous exercise exactly but now raise your head toward your knees and gently rock back and forth. Release. Relax and repeat four to six times.

5. Still on the floor, bend your knees, lift your head off the floor and drop your chin toward your chest. Curl up, using your stomach muscles. Keep them contracted and pulled in. When all vertebrae have cleared the floor—you will be in a near sitting position—slowly lower yourself, vertebra by vertebra, back down to starting position. Repeat five times, building up to ten.

6. If your back or abdominal muscles are very weak, try a variation of the exercise above. Lie on your back with ankles crossed and arms crossed on chest. Bring your knees up until your feet are well clear of the floor. Curl your head and shoulders toward the knees. Hold. Repeat five to ten times.

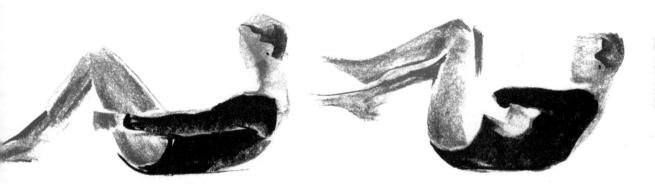

7. Exercise #5 can be made more difficult simply by folding your arms behind your head and then curling up.

8. Check with your doctor before doing this one if you have a back problem. Lie on your stomach with heels together, forehead touching the floor. Place your hands with palms down next to your shoulders. Slowly raise your chest off the floor. Lift your spine. Look upward and stretch your neck and head back. Keep your pelvic bones in touch with the floor at all times. Hold. Lower your chest back to the floor. Repeat two to three times.

9. Lie on your stomach, legs straight out in back. Place your chin on your hands. Lift your right leg as high as possible, but keep your hip bones touching the floor at all times. Hold. Lower your leg. Repeat three to five times for each leg.

10. Get down on your hands and knees, with your weight evenly distributed. Stretch out your right hand and arm and your left leg until they are fully extended. Lift the extended arm and leg together until they are even with your body. Hold. Return arm and leg to starting position. Repeat with other arm and leg. Do each twice.

FOR THE LEGS

1. Sit on the floor, legs straight out in front. Place your right leg over your left leg. Press down with your right leg and up with your left. Hold. Release. Reverse your legs. Do three times in each position.

2. Stand. Bend your right knee, raising your leg toward your chest. Wrap your arms around the knee and gently pull toward your body as far as you can. Hold. Repeat with left leg. Do two times for each.

3. With the left hand, hold on to the back of a chair or a table about waist high for support. Raise your right leg straight out in front of you as high as possible. Hold. Swing your leg to the side. Hold. Return foot to the floor. Repeat with left leg. Do three times with each leg.

4. Stand with your feet about two feet apart. Bend your right knee and gently lunge to the right side, keeping your knee bent and your right foot pointing to the side. Hold. Release. Reverse legs. Repeat three to five times on each side.

When you have completed your exercises, lie on the floor on your back and practice your breathing exercises—very gently, easily and evenly.

It is better to practice *some* exercises every day than to go for days doing nothing.

Using Weights or Dumbbells

Using very light weights (or "heavy hand" weights) can be very helpful in firming and toning muscles, particularly in the least exercised and more fragile upper half of the body. Weights also help with your breathing exercises. They increase the amount of air you can bring into your lungs as well as firm and strengthen the upper arm areas.

Start by using three-pound weights. You'll be able to stay with these for some time unless you are in very good shape at the beginning. You will never need anything heavier than a five-pound dumbbell. Do six to ten repetitions for each exercise, gradually building up to about fifteen to twenty repetitions. Twenty is near maximum for results with a specific weight. After that, you may want to increase the weight of the dumbbell, or stay with what you are using and keep the status quo. Don't overdo. It's best to build up muscle strength slowly. Exercise with dumbbells every other day to allow your muscles time to recover from the workout.

You'll be holding the dumbbells in two basic positions. The *overhand* position is when the fingers face away from the body with the wrists turned out. The *underhand* position is when your fingers face *in* toward your body.

EXERCISES USING LIGHT WEIGHTS

For the upper body, shoulders and chest muscles: Lying on the floor, hold a dumbbell in each hand in the underhand position, arms at your sides. Inhale and raise the dumbbells straight over your head to touch the floor behind you. Keep your elbows straight. Exhale as you slowly raise and swing the dumbbells back over your head to your sides. Repeat.

For the chest muscles: Lie on the floor, holding the dumbbells in an underhand position, arms at right angles to the body. Exhale as you slowly bring the dumbbells together over your head. Inhale as you return the dumbbells to the floor. Repeat.

For the backs of the arms: Lie on the floor, holding the dumbbells in an overhand position. Your elbows are bent, with the dumbbells resting over each shoulder. Inhale. Slowly press up until your arms are fully extended. Exhale as you return the dumbbells to starting position. Repeat.

For the thighs: Stand in front of a straight chair with your back to the chair and feet shoulder width apart. Hold the dumbbells in an underhand position at shoulder level, elbows bent. Bend your knees until you reach sitting position. Sit. Raise yourself slowly to standing position. Repeat.

For the back, shoulders and arms: Standing, hold the dumbbells in an overhand position, hands down at your sides. Slowly raise the dumbbells up over your head as high as you can reach. Keep your back straight as you do this. Return the dumbbells slowly to starting position. Repeat.

For the arms: Standing, hold the dumbbells in an underhand position. Raise the dumbbells to your shoulders but keep your elbows down. Return your hands slowly to starting position. Repeat.

For the arms: Stand and hold the dumbbells in an overhand position, arms down and hands in front of your thighs. Raise your hands to just under your chin, then press your arms out directly in front of you to their full extension. Return your arms to starting position. This should be done as a continuous motion. Do it slowly, establishing an even pace, as if you were rowing. Repeat.

For the back and the backs of the arms: Stand holding the dumbbell in an overhand position, arms at your sides. Bend at your waist, keeping your back straight. Raise your arms up behind you as far as possible. Count to ten. Release and return hands to starting position. Repeat.

Aerobic Exercises—to Prime Your Pump!

Aerobics work your major body muscles, the ones that move you, especially your legs and buttocks. As you do aerobic exercises, your muscles will gain a new lease on life. You can also burn off twice as many calories doing aerobics as doing other exercises. And sufficient exercise, not just flailing around for a couple of minutes, acts as a natural appetite suppressor.

You need aerobics to prime your pump—literally. As you grow older, your heart-lung function declines if you do not stimulate it. And limited heart-lung function can limit your life. Aerobics gets your machinery working and keeps it working.

What's more, aerobics can help your mental attitude change from a depressed, negative state of mind to a positive one. Studies done on clinically depressed people show that after three weeks of a program of walking, jogging or running, their depression is gone. It has also been demonstrated that people who work out, with their heart rate at approximately 60 percent of its maximum, release a hormone known as norepinephrine, which is related to happy attitudes and feelings and helps do away with depression. All this from fifteen to twenty minutes of aerobic exercise!

You should keep in mind the following things about aerobic exercise.

- Aerobic action consists of continuing muscle action that generates an elevated pulse rate for a sustained period of time. To find the pulse rate that is right for you, subtract your age from 220 and take 70 percent of that. If you are forty-five years old, that would be 220 minus 45 (175) times 70 percent, or a pulse rate of 120. You want to get your pulse rate up to 120 beats per minute and keep it there for fifteen to thirty minutes. (During the course of your exercise, check your pulse rate every ten minutes or so. If you are over the target rate, you should slow down.)
- You must exercise a minimum of three times a week, allowing forty-eight hours between strenuous sessions.
- You must exercise a minimum of fifteen minutes each workout session. Your goal should be twenty to forty-five minutes, including time to warm up and cool down (about ten minutes each).
- Increase your workout time by building slowly. In the beginning, alternate your exercise with periods of walking. Remember that a body that has not been exercised will tire from the simplest effort. If this happens, slow down, but keep on going!

I have a jump rope hanging in my closet. If I had room for a small trampoline, I would have that, too. And I have my own two feet for jogging or walking in place. Or I go outdoors for a walk, jog or run, or all three in combination, trying to stay in continuous motion and to sustain a heart rate higher than normal. Swimming and cross-country skiing are also excellent aerobic exercises, but obviously you need to be in a special place or have a pool available to do these often.

I am an early riser, and because I was brought up in the country, I gravitate to the outdoors, preferring to be outside when I can. When the weather permits, I often pull on my sweat clothes and running shoes and go out to jog-walk for fifteen or twenty minutes. This affords me another pleasure—I can participate in the dawning day. No two dawns are alike, and for me, the relative quiet of the early mornings is a joy that transcends the idea of just exercise.

WALKING: THE EASIEST AEROBIC EXERCISE

To get aerobic benefits from walking, you must walk actively, aware of the movements of your body. For me, walking has become a game that is fun whether I am in the city or in the country. I walk creatively, inventively. I am aware of the movements of my hips, thighs, feet. I tense different muscles in my thighs, buttocks, abdomen or arms as I go along. I've learned to feel what they do and the effects I can create.

Pay special attention to your posture as you walk. Notice your back. How straight is it? I recognized that I did not always have a straight spine, but had a tendency to buckle slightly in the middle, which affected my stomach and shoulders. Straightening your spine, stretching it tall, pulling in your abdomen and setting your shoulders straight will lift your lung and chest areas to where they belong. You will breathe better. Your muscles and your lungs will work better for you.

I *feel* my stride. I experiment with changes—longer, shorter, faster, slower and all possible combinations. I move my hips more and less. You can start out by varying the speed of your stride, walking fast for a minute or two, then slowly for the next minute. Keep repeating that pattern, eventually walking at your faster pace for longer and longer intervals. (You can walk in place at home, repeating the same sort of pattern.)

One of the simplest ways to know when your heart rate is elevated and you are getting aerobic benefits is by your breathing. When your breathing intensifies (not to the point of panting, though, just breathing harder than you're used to), you are "with it."

Walk a mile a day. Time yourself. The goal is to be able to walk your mile in just under fifteen minutes. At that rate you will get the maximum aerobic rate from walking. And that fifteen-minute fast walk will burn off 140 calories!

CYCLING

Stationary bikes are terrific, particularly for exercise during the cold months and on rainy days when I know I don't want to go outdoors. I also do not like biking in New York City traffic. The iron steed awaits.

My bike is at the back of my room, and a television is in the front. I watch the morning or evening news while pedaling away. It helps. Or I turn on music. That helps, too.

After I set the level of resistance, I pedal for about twelve minutes, gradually increasing my rate of speed until the speedometer reads between 15 and 20 miles per hour. If the resistance level seems too low, I increase it, but I pedal to maintain the same rate of speed until my time runs out.

Beginners should start with resistance set at zero and systematically increase it little by little. Your leg muscles will tell you what is enough. You will feel it and know immediately.

How long you can sustain a rate of speed depends on your condition and muscle tone, but the greater your speed for a given length of time, the greater your aerobic benefits. A basic goal should be fifteen minutes. As you develop strength and stamina, increase both resistance and speed.

As you complete your riding time, turn the resistance down gradually and slow to a stop, letting your heart rate subside. Walk around the room for a minute or two if your legs feel rubbery after you finish. It wears off fast.

As for all exercise, doing it is what counts, even if you ride your bike for only five, seven or ten minutes a day at first. Do whatever you can tolerate— but start!

JUMPING ROPE

I used to be able to jump rope by the hour (or so it seemed). Today it is by the minute. Jumping rope is another aerobic exercise that can be done inside or outside. All you need is a rope and a good pair of cushioned sneakers. And a support bra if you have medium or full breasts. GO!

Jumping rope is excellent for coordination. It also gets your heart going in a hurry. And it strengthens all the major muscle groups, arms and shoulders as well as leg muscles. Jump on a cushioned surface when possible, even if you are wearing your sneakers, and keep your arms close to your body.

In the beginning, alternate your jumping time with intervals of rest time. If you jump for fifteen seconds, then rest by walking around or in place for thirty or even forty seconds. Repeat this routine about eight times. After a week, reduce your rest time and increase the number of sequences you do to ten or twelve. In another week, increase your jumping time to thirty seconds. Eventually, you will be able to jump for two or three minutes before resting.

Build up to as much uninterrupted jumping time as you can handle. Remember to go slowly, but stay at it for the minimum fifteen minutes. Ten minutes of jumping is equal to thirty minutes of jogging.

SWIMMING

Swimming is one of the best aerobic exercises for everyone. Unfortunately, it is not always convenient. It is also the gentlest exercise on your body frame because being suspended in water removes all strains on your joints, which normally act like springs to absorb the impact from your motions. If you suffer from stiff joints or arthritis, swimming may be the best medicine around, and I think it is worth going to almost any length or inconvenience to find a pool to exercise in.

To get aerobic benefits from swimming, you should swim at a sustained speed for fifteen or twenty minutes at a crack. If you just stay in the water for that time, moving at a slower pace, kicking your legs and moving your arms about, even doing water exercises, that's okay, but it's not aerobic and won't give you the same benefits.

Relatively few people have the stamina, endurance and strength to swim for a sustained fifteen minutes. It's a goal to work toward if you have a place to swim and can work out regularly.

JOGGING OR JOG-WALKING

Put on your running shoes. Now you can either jog in place indoors or go outside. Beginners should alternate jogging with walking. As you build stamina and endurance, increase your jogging time until you can jog for a straight fifteen minutes. The combination of walking and jogging is effective as long as you stay in motion for a minimum of fifteen minutes. It doesn't matter if you walk more than you jog for a while. What does matter is that you are out there moving.

You're Not Finished Yet! Sink Stretches

My bathroom, which is very small, also serves as my personal mini-gym. After I shower, my sink turns into an exercise bar. I have discovered that most sinks are the same height, and any sink can become an exercise bar.

When I dry myself, I place one foot on the edge of the sink. Keeping my leg straight, I slowly reach for my toes, stretching as far as I can and at the same time bringing my head down to my knee. I hold that position for ten seconds. I do this twice and repeat with the other leg.

While I have my foot up on the sink, I flex it a few times, and then take my hands and push my toes forward and back. Both legs and feet get dried this way, too.

Then I place one hand on the edge of the sink and do a few knee bends, but going down only to a near sitting position and then up again, keeping my back very straight. I do six to ten of these.

Holding the edge of the sink, I raise myself up and down on my toes as many as twenty times to exercise my whole foot or feet. These exercises can be done in rapid succession.

Still holding on, I lift one foot up behind me, grab hold of it and press it in toward my buttocks, counting to ten. Then I repeat with the other leg.

Placing both hands on the edge of the sink, I tighten my buttocks and with my leg straight lift my right foot off the floor, raising it up and down behind me in short rapid lifts. I do this as many times as I can stand it—and then do a couple more. I repeat with my left leg.

Exercise can be done almost anywhere and anytime. But you have to develop an exercise consciousness. Then you will find, create, use, make opportunities for yourself to move your body, regardless of the time and place!

Isometric Exercises: Your Discreet Friends

The following exercises can be done wherever you are throughout the day. They can be particularly helpful if you are obliged to sit for long periods without moving about. (Remember these when you're stuck on an airplane or taking a long automobile trip.) Hold each exercise for a slow count of six to ten seconds.

If you are standing around waiting for something—water to boil, an elevator to come, a red light to change, an appointment, a movie line to proceed— contract! Contract your abdominal muscles. Hold. Release. Repeat at least ten times. Do the same with vaginal and buttock muscles. Every muscle needs toning and strengthening. And remember your back, your posture and your breathing.

If you are standing in a doorway (like your closet doorway when you're deciding what to wear), place the backs of your hands against the door sides and press. Hold.

Reach overhead and place your hands against the door frame and press. Hold.

Take a minute and lock your hands in front of your chest and pull. Hold. Reverse your hand position. Then push your hands together and hold.

If you are sitting, keep both feet on the floor, hands on your knees. Pull in your abdomen and press down hard on your knees. Hold. Release.

With hands on your knees, try to lift your heels off the floor. Resist. Hold.

With your knees shoulder width apart, place your hands outside of each knee. Press in with your hands. Resist with the knees. Hold.

Hold on to the sides of your chair and attempt to raise the chair. Resist. Hold.

At your desk, place your hands palms down on top of the desk. Press. Hold. Place palms flat against the underside of the desk. Push. Hold.

When you need to stretch your leg muscles while still sitting, put one leg out in front of you, pull your stomach in tightly, and rotate your foot ten times in each direction. Repeat with the other leg.

Put one leg out in front of you, raise it six to seven inches off the floor and hold. Repeat with the other leg.

"Help! I Still Can't Get Started . . ."

Making that commitment to exercise every single day is often the greatest challenge, especially if you are not active in any sports, are seriously out of shape or have not exercised in years. Sometimes you have to *trick* yourself into a routine by starting *very* gradually, with a short daily walk, easing into a few stretches, adding some yoga or isometrics, then finally doing an aerobic activity. You may have to sneak up on an exercise routine.

But this bears repeating and repeating: It is important that exercise become a part of your life, like brushing your teeth. You are not exercising just to get in shape. You are setting up a habit to follow *every day* of your life. Don't stop just because you have lost a few pounds or trimmed a few inches from your trouble spots.

It's fine to get outside help. In fact, if you have not exercised for years—or *ever*—you should find someone to work with you one-on-one in the beginning. You need the encouragement, the individual attention and a very gradual transition to this new way of life.

Check with a doctor before you begin your program. He or she should be able to tell you how much exercise you can do at this point. Your doctor may also recommend a physiotherapist, a particular instructor or a program to follow that is safe for you.

Then try to book at least one private session with your instructor to familiarize yourself with the routine, to check your body position (there is a right and a wrong way to every exercise) and to get to know your limits—when to stop.

Most of us have signed up for a health club or a series of classes and gotten bogged down halfway through. Perhaps the class was too strenuous, monotonous or impersonal. In any case, it was a chore and often a bore. With exercise classes, so much depends on the quality of the instructor and your rapport with him or her that I recommend you take trial classes everywhere in town until you find an instructor you like personally. If you can't relate to the instructor, you probably won't enjoy and continue the classes.

A good class should make you feel energized, not exhausted. Afterward, your muscles should have a *good* tired feeling, like they have been used, not abused. You may feel stiff and sore the next day, but you should never feel pain.

Another point: Don't get competitive in class. You are there to work your body, not to give a performance. Never feel you have to do everything everyone else in class does. You may only be able to do a few exercises at first. Know your limits and build up gradually. Be sure to alert the instructor ahead of time about any physical problems you may have, especially back and knee problems, so she can tell you which exercises to avoid.

Make Your Vacation a Time to Improve Your Body

Too often we need a vacation from our vacation. We come back tanned and rested, but also overindulged, with a few extra pounds. Why not rethink your vacation time and use it to build up your health and your body? Plan it around learning a new sport, taking long walks in beautiful scenery or reevaluating your exercise regime with the help of experts.

There are many health and beauty-oriented resorts where you'll find a team of experts at your disposal. They can give you the boost you need to get started, as well as a custom-tailored plan that fits your specific needs. You can try out different types of exercise under close supervision—most spas offer everything from aerobics to yoga and water exercises. If you have not had the time to investigate a variety of exercises, here's your opportunity.

The pampering massages and skin treatments offered at some of the more luxurious spas are a reason in themselves for going. But the real reason for blitzing your body with a week of exercise, diet and pampering is to give yourself the incentive to continue at home. And to give yourself a complete program to take with you. (Some spas even supply exercise tapes.) So think about a health spa as a vacation alternative.

Another plus: Spas are great places to vacation *alone*. You'll never be lonely or bored, for there are lots of congenial companions. And you'll return looking gorgeous and revitalized.

Exercise and the Working Woman

If you're a working woman, you have a hundred excuses not to exercise, beginning with "I have no time." Does it help for me to say that planned exercises that work every muscle in your body will give you *more* time and *more* energy?

In fact, you must exercise, particularly if you have a sedentary job. Bad posture (the result of slumping at your desk or of weakened abdominal muscles), spreading hips and thighs are only the outward signs. Internally, poor circulation, backaches, the many manifestations of stress and tension, and frequent headaches are some of the ailments exercise can help. Whether you are working up to a place of prominence or starting fresh in the working world, you have to *train* for it physically as well as mentally.

I am a great advocate of walking—everywhere. When I see young executive women in running shoes, briefcases in hand, walking to work, I think how wise they are to make the very best use of their travel time. Why not you, too? If your office is a mile or two away, that's walking distance. Or you can walk part of the way. It's a great way to clear your head before the day's business or walk off your tension afterward. (Don't fall into the trap of easing your tension with an alcoholic drink—that only adds calories and could get you into a very destructive habit.)

Sneak in some exercise on the job. Isometric exercises like the ones I've described are excellent exercises to do at your desk. Upper-body stretches,

185

head rolls, arm and shoulder circles are other ways to work out the kinks from sitting in one position. Many companies are installing gyms and jogging trails to encourage fitness. Take advantage of them whenever you can. They are not just for junior executives, they're for you, too!

If you work in a high-stress job, make exercise a complete change of pace. Try a fun, playful activity (you don't need more work!) like dancing, racketball, even roller-skating. There is a sport you can learn, regardless of your age.

Exercise is not more work, it's more *play!*

Your Equipment: Treat Yourself Right

Giving yourself good equipment means you're taking your fitness program seriously. And good equipment doesn't mean buying a complete home gym. It just means setting things up so that it is easy to exercise; giving yourself every possible advantage.

The right footwear: This should be your priority. Badly fitting footwear can seriously hamper your performance and lead to knee and back problems, not to mention corns and blisters. Your athletic shoes absorb impact and cushion shock waves that would otherwise travel the length of your spine.

Most sports shoes are tailored for a specific kind of activity. You won't find one shoe that works equally well for jogging, tennis, aerobics and racketball. Look for a shoe designed for your specific sport and then have an expert fit you according to your foot (the best running shoe for your foot may not be the newest model that's "in" with marathoners). Find the nearest sports shoe store where serious runners go. The fitter will find the shoe and the size that's right for your foot and your activity and suggest the socks to go with it.

Here's what to look for in a good sports shoe:

- The fit at the heel and toe. There should be plenty of room in front to wiggle your toes. The heel fit should be snug, but not tight.
- Support. You should have good support at the arches, particularly if you have foot problems.
- Enough but not too much cushioning. The cushioning you need depends on the surface you'll be running or playing on. You need protection from impact, but enough contact with the surface to keep your balance.

Another alternative—and a good idea if you have problem feet—is to go to a sports podiatrist. This doctor can create a mold of the bottom of your foot to slip into your shoes (which works well in any kind of casual footwear, too) to give you the ideal balance and support. These molds, called orthotics, can make a world of difference in your performance and enjoyment of any activity, including simple walking.

A good support bra: Bouncing and jiggling from jogging and aerobics can stretch the ligaments of the breasts and cause them to sag. To avoid this, you should wear a sports bra for support. There are many good ones on the market. This is very important if you have full breasts.

Exercise clothes: These are an option. You can really exercise in anything that gives you freedom of movement. But psychologically, attractive exercise clothes are very important. You'll want to exercise more if you look good, if you're wearing an up color, if you feel you're dressed right for that activity. (Who wants to don baggy old sweats every day? They can make you feel even more out of shape!) So get yourself some inexpensive exercise clothes that spell "fun"—lavender leotards, a fire-engine red warmup suit, a crisp tennis dress—and a lightweight nylon tote in which to carry them with you.

Floor mats: Exercises done on the floor, particularly yoga, require a padded surface to cushion your spine. Unless you have a very thick carpet, you need a floor mat. A roll of one-inch-thick foam rubber about two and a half feet by four feet works just fine. Or you can buy a special vinyl-covered exercise mat.

Weights: For the weight exercises I recommend, you need only a pair of two-, three- or five-pound weights. You can buy these dumbbells in sporting goods stores.

Jump rope, exercise bicycle, trampoline, rowing machine, tummy rollers, etc.: There is an endless list of exercise gadgets on the market today. Some are very useful, others can cause dangerous muscle strains. If you are starting out, it's always best to use your body's own natural resistance. Check with your exercise instructor or doctor before you use any gadget or gizmo that could strain your muscles. Be especially careful of the kind of weights you attach to running shoes. They can stress your ankles and knees.

Be well equipped. Keep your exercise equipment handy, easy to use, fun and right for what you're doing. You should be able to get yourself together for a workout without a second thought.

Setting Up Your Own Exercise Class at Home

If you have a video cassette recorder and cable television, you can set up your own exercise classes at home. Look in your television listings for the many exercise programs now on the air. Tape a few and review them at your leisure. Some will be far too difficult; others just challenging enough. You can put together a tape of your favorites to use during your exercise time.

I suggest starting with one of the excellent yoga programs. They're gentle, relaxing and not likely to overtax you. Then add more strenuous exercises and a mild aerobic workout.

If you like exercise classes but somehow never get to one, these video workouts are made for you. (And now you have no excuse to miss a class!) You can exercise any time of day that's convenient. You can invite a few friends over for a taped workout. You do miss the specialized attention that you get in a good class, and if you push yourself too hard with a video class, there is no one there to warn you not to overdo, but if you can read your body signals and know when to quit, then using your own exercise tape could be the best way to get in your regular exercise time.

There are now commercially prepared tapes aimed at the older woman's exercise needs. These are also an excellent way to get into the exercise habit. But first review the tape carefully. Again, know your body and don't strain it. Learn to feel the difference between the slightly uncomfortable "burn" of a muscle that is being worked fully and the pain that tells you to stop immediately.

One of the best things about setting up an exercise program at home, one you can always do whenever you want, is the independence it gives you. But freedom requires discipline to accomplish anything. You and you alone are responsible for getting your full workout. Sometimes you may not be in the mood, and it's easy to cop out. Here's how to be sure to get your exercise time in:

- Set a time every day for your exercise "class" and be sure to do *some* kind of exercise, regardless of how you feel. Even if it's just a few stretches. Get your body used to wanting exercise at that time.
- If you are feeling very tired or out of sorts, do just a few posture and breathing exercises. Then take a long walk.
- Wear happy, brightly colored clothes to exercise in. Get exercise clothes you'll look forward to wearing.
- Make a tape of your favorite upbeat songs to play while you exercise.
- Vary your routine every day.

188

• Develop a repertoire of exercises for every part of the body, so you can change your routines and not get bored.

Make your exercise time enjoyable, sociable, fun. But take responsibility for it yourself. You should not depend on an exercise instructor or a gym to keep you in shape. By putting together your own routine and getting your body used to moving and stretching frequently, you'll have your exercise life well under control.

The responsibility for your well-being is yours.

It's your body.

You have information and tools with which to work.

Build a program to fit your life and personality.

It is for you to know that you are Always Beautiful.